COMPLETE
Cake Decorating

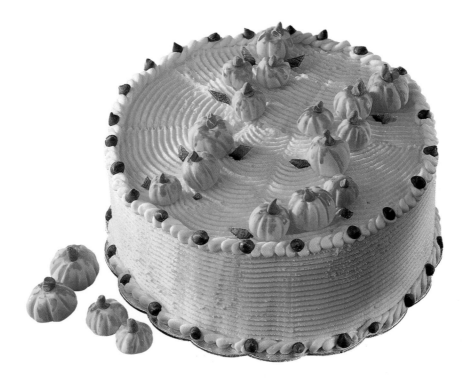

COMPLETE
Cake Decorating

Techniques, Basic Recipes and
Beautiful Cake Projects for all Occasions

Angela Nilsen & Sarah Maxwell

Photography by Tim Hill

LORENZ BOOKS

This edition published in 1998 by Lorenz Books

LORENZ BOOKS are available for bulk purchase for sales promotion
and for premium use. For details, write or call the sales director,
Lorenz Books, 27 West 20th Street, New York, NY 10011;
(800) 354-9657

© Anness Publishing Limited

Lorenz Books is an imprint of
Anness Publishing Inc.

This edition distributed in Canada by Raincoast Books
8680 Cambie Street, Vancouver, British Columbia V6P 6M9

ISBN 1-85967-037-7

Publisher: Joanna Lorenz
Project Editor: Judith Simons
Photographer: Tim Hill
Home Economists: Angela Nilsen and Sarah Maxwell
Assistant Home Economist: Teresa Goldfinch
Stylist: Sarah Maxwell
Assistant Stylist: Timna Rose
Design: Axis Design

Printed in Singapore by Star Standard Industries Pte. Ltd.

1 3 5 7 9 10 8 6 4 2

Contents

Introduction 7

Basic Cake Recipes 8

Basic Icing Recipes 20

Covering Cakes 30

Decorating with Royal Icing 36

Decorating with Sugarpaste Icing 44

Decorating with Marzipan 52

Decorating with Butter Icing 58

Decorating with Glacé Icing 62

Decorating with Chocolate 66

Using Bought Decorations 74

Classic Cakes 83

Special Occasion Cakes 105

Children's Novelty Cakes 129

Index 158

Acknowledgements 160

Introduction

Complete Cake Decorating is not only an invaluable foundation course in cake decorating techniques, but is also a wonderful reference book for a host of tried-and-tested recipes for classic cake bases and icings, as well as inspirational cake projects, which you will use again and again.

Clearly structured, the decorating course leads you through all the different decorating techniques which can be applied to royal icing, sugarpaste, marzipan, chocolate and other icings. There are step-by-step instructions and photographs for piping, crimping, embossing, frills, plaques, coloring, run-outs, modeling, stenciling, flowers, using purchased decorations, such as sweet confections, ribbons and fresh flowers, and much more.

The wonderful decorated cakes featured in the project sections on Classic Cakes, Special Occasion Cakes, and Children's Novelty Cakes are a feast for the eye and palate. Moreover, they provide wonderful working examples which you can follow step-by-step, giving you the opportunity to practice and develop the techniques described in the first section of the book with professional results.

Do follow each recipe as closely as possible. Baking is one area of cooking in which accuracy will greatly improve the likelihood of achieving good results. When whisking egg whites, make sure the bowl and whisk are perfectly clean. For best results, use eggs at room temperature. If you sift flour from a height, it will have more chance to aerate and lighten.

No two ovens are alike. If possible, buy a reliable oven thermometer and test the temperature of your oven. Always bake in the center of the oven where the heat is more likely to be constant. If using a fan assisted oven, follow the manufacturer's guidelines for baking. Good quality cake pans will also improve results, as they conduct heat more efficiently.

Finally, there are some current health concerns about the use of raw egg in uncooked recipes. Homemade royal icing, marzipan and sugarpaste icing do include raw egg. An alternative recipe for royal icing, using pure albumen powder, has been provided in light of this. If you prefer to avoid raw egg, do buy ready-made marzipan and sugarpaste. Store-bought versions are usually good quality products and are, of course, very quick and easy to use.

Basic Cake Recipes

Cakes are the highlight of many celebrations. What birthday would be complete without a cake with candles to blow out, or a wedding without a beautiful cake to cut? Some of the most traditional cake recipes provide the best bases for decorating. Recipes can be found in this chapter, and are used as bases for the decorated cakes later in the book. None of the cakes involve complicated techniques, and several are as simple as putting the ingredients into a bowl, and mixing them together.

Fruit cake is one of the most popular special occasion cakes. Among its advantages is that it keeps really well and in fact improves with storage, so it can be baked well ahead of time and decorated in easy stages. It also provides a wonderfully firm base for all sorts of elegant or novelty decorations. There are other ideas, too, for those who prefer a less rich tasting cake, such as the Madeira or a light fruit cake, as well as a quick-mix sponge for those last-minute, spontaneous celebrations.

Baking Equipment

A selection of basic equipment is needed for successful cake making. The following are a few of the more necessary items:

Scales For good, consistent results, ingredients for cake making require precise measuring. An accurate set of scales is therefore essential.

Bowls Various sizes of glass or china heatproof bowls with rounded sides make mixing easier and are useful when baking.

Measuring Cup A glass measuring cup is easy to read and means liquids are calculated accurately.

Measuring Spoons These are available in a standard size, making the measuring of small amounts more accurate.

Sifters These are used to aerate flour before baking, making cakes lighter in texture, and to remove lumps from confectioners' sugar or cocoa powder.

Electric Beaters These are particularly useful for whisking egg whites for jelly rolls.

Balloon Whisks Useful for beating smaller amounts of either egg or cream mixtures.

Waxed Paper Used to line cake pans to prevent cakes from sticking.

Wooden and Metal Spoons Wooden

spoons in various sizes are essential for beating mixtures together when not using electric beaters, while metal spoons are necessary for folding in ingredients and for smoothing over mixtures to give a flat surface before baking.

Spatulas Because they are so pliable, plastic spatulas are particularly useful for scraping all the cake mixture from a bowl.

Cake Pans These are available in all shapes and sizes, and the thicker the metal the less likely the cake will be to overcook. Most cake icing specialists rent cake pans, useful when very large or unusual shaped pans are required.

Oven Gloves Essential when removing anything hot from the oven. It is worth choosing a good quality, well lined pair of gloves.

Wire Racks Made from wire mesh, these are available in different sizes and shapes and allow cakes to "breathe" as they cool.

Cake Boards Choose the shape and size to fit the cake. Thick boards are for large, heavy cakes, royal iced cakes and any other fruit cake coated in icing. The board should be 2 inches larger than the size of the cake. Thinner boards are for small Madeira cakes and other lighter cakes covered with icings such as butter, glacé or fudge. These can be about 1 inch larger than the cake size.

1 glass mixing bowls
2 balloon whisk
3 large round cake pan
4 electric beaters
5 small round cake pan
6 scales
7 large square cake pan
8 measuring cup
9 measuring spoons
10 cake boards
11 pastry brush
12 pre-cut waxed paper pan liners
13 scissors
14 wooden mixing spoons
15 wire rack
16 sifter
17 oven gloves
18 plastic spatula

Quick-mix Sponge Cake

Here's a no-fuss, foolproof all-in-one cake, where the ingredients are quickly mixed together. The following quantities and baking instructions are for a deep 8 inch round cake pan or an 8 inch ring mold. For other quantities and pan sizes, follow the baking instructions given in the decorated cake recipes.

INGREDIENTS
1 cup self-rising flour
1 tsp baking powder
½ cup soft margarine
½ cup superfine sugar
2 large eggs

STORING AND FREEZING
The cake can be made up to two days in advance, wrapped in plastic wrap or foil and stored in an airtight container. The cake can be frozen for up to three months.

FLAVORINGS
The following amounts are for a 2-egg, single quantity cake, as above. Increase the amounts proportionally for larger cakes.
Chocolate Fold 1 tbsp cocoa powder blended with 1 tbsp boiling water into the cake mixture.
Citrus Fold 2 tsp of finely grated lemon, orange or lime zest into the cake mixture.

1 Preheat the oven to 325°F. Grease the round cake pan, line the base with waxed paper and then grease the paper, or grease and flour the ring mold.

2 ▲ Sift the flour and baking powder into a bowl. Add the margarine, sugar and eggs.

3 ▲ Beat with a wooden spoon for 2–3 minutes. The mixture should be pale in color and slightly glossy.

4 Spoon the cake mixture into the prepared pan and then smooth the surface. Bake for 20–30 minutes. To test if cooked, press the cake lightly in the center. If firm, the cake is done, if soft, cook for a little longer. Alternatively, insert a skewer into the center of the cake. If it comes out clean the cake is ready. Turn out on to a wire rack, remove the lining paper and leave to cool completely.

This quick-mix sponge cake can be filled and simply decorated with icing for a special occasion.

Jelly Roll

Jelly rolls are traditionally made without fat, so they don't keep as long as most other cakes. However, they have a deliciously light texture and provide the cook with the potential for all sorts of luscious fillings and tasty toppings.

6 ▲ Pour the cake mixture into the prepared pan and then smooth the surface, being careful not to press out any air.

7 Bake in the center of the oven for 12–15 minutes. To test if cooked, press lightly in the center. If the cake springs back it is done. It will also start to come away from the edges of the pan.

8 Turn the cake out on to a piece of waxed paper lightly sprinkled with superfine sugar. Peel off the lining paper and cut off any crisp edges of the cake with a sharp knife. Spread with jam or jelly, if wished, and roll up, using the waxed paper as a guide. Leave to cool on a wire rack.

Vary the flavor of a traditional jelly roll by adding a little grated orange, lime or lemon rind to the basic mixture.

INGREDIENTS
4 large eggs, separated
½ cup superfine sugar
1 cup flour
1 tsp baking powder

STORING AND FREEZING
Jelly rolls and other fat-free sponges do not keep well, so if possible bake on the day of eating. Otherwise, wrap in plastic wrap or foil and store in an airtight container overnight or freeze for up to three months.

4 ▼ Carefully fold the beaten egg yolks into the egg white mixture with a metal spoon.

5 Sift together the flour and baking powder. Carefully fold the flour mixture into the egg mixture with a metal spoon.

1 Preheat the oven to 350°F. Grease a 13 x 9 inch jelly roll pan, line with waxed paper and grease the paper.

2 Whisk the egg whites in a clean, dry bowl until stiff. Beat in 2 tbsp of the sugar.

3 ▲ Place the egg yolks, remaining sugar and 1 tbsp water in a bowl and beat for about 2 minutes until the mixture is pale and leaves a thick trail when the beaters are lifted.

adeira Cake

This fine-textured cake makes a good base for decorating and is therefore a useful alternative to fruit cake, although it will not keep as long. It provides a firmer, longer-lasting base than a Victoria sponge, and can be covered with butter icing, fudge frosting, a thin layer of marzipan or sugarpaste icing. For the ingredients, decide what size and shape of cake you wish to make and then follow the chart shown opposite.

STORING AND FREEZING
The cake can be made up to a week in advance, wrapped in plastic wrap or foil and stored in an airtight container. The cake can be frozen for up to three months.

Madeira cake provides a firmer base for icing than a Victoria sponge. It can be covered with a thin layer of sugarpaste, as here, or marzipan, and is a great alternative for anyone who does not like fruit cake.

1 Preheat the oven to 325°F. Grease a deep cake pan, line the base and sides with a double thickness of waxed paper and then lightly grease the paper.

2 ▲ Sift together the flour and baking powder into a mixing bowl. Add the margarine, sugar, eggs and lemon juice.

3 ▲ Stir the ingredients together with a wooden spoon until they are all well combined.

4 ▲ Beat the mixture for about 2 minutes until smooth and glossy.

5 Spoon the mixture into the prepared pan and smooth the top. Bake in the center of the oven, following the chart opposite as a guide for baking times. If the cake browns too quickly, cover the top loosely with foil. To test if baked, press lightly in the center. If the cake springs back it is done. Alternatively, test by inserting a skewer into the center of the cake. If it comes out clean the cake is done. Leave the cake to cool in the pan for 5 minutes and then turn out on to a wire rack. Remove the lining paper and leave to cool.

MADEIRA CAKE CHART

Cake pan sizes	7 in round	8 in round	9 in round	10 in round	12 in round
	6 in square	7 in square	8 in square	9 in square	11 in square
Flour	2 cups	3 cups	4 cups	4½ cups	6 cups
Baking powder	1½ tsp	2 tsp	2½ tsp	1 tbsp	4 tsp
Soft margarine	¾ cup	1¼ cups	1½ cups	1¾ cups	2¼ cups
Superfine sugar	¾ cup	1¼ cups	1½ cups	1¾ cups	2½ cups
Eggs, large, beaten	3	4	6	7	10
Lemon juice	1 tbsp	1½ tbsp	2 tbsp	2½ tbsp	4 tbsp
Approx. baking time	1¼ – 1½ hours	1½ – 1¾ hours	1¾ – 2 hours	1¾ – 2 hours	2¼ – 2½ hours

A traditional Madeira cake peaks and cracks slightly on the top. For a flat surface on which to ice, simply level the top with a sharp knife.

Rich Fruit Cake

This is the traditional cake mixture for many cakes made for special occasions such as weddings, Christmas, anniversaries and christenings. Make the cake a few weeks before icing, keep it well wrapped and stored in an airtight container and it should mature beautifully. Because of all its rich ingredients, this fruit cake will keep moist and fresh for several months. Follow the ingredients guide in the chart opposite for the size of cake you wish to make.

STORING

When the cake is cold, wrap in a double thickness of waxed paper or foil. Store in an airtight container in a cool dry place where it will keep for several months. During storage, the cake can be unwrapped and the bottom brushed with brandy (about half the amount used in the recipe). Re-wrap before storing again. As the cake keeps so well, there is no need to freeze.

A long-lasting cake which is full of rich flavors.

1 Preheat the oven to 275°F. Grease a deep cake pan, line the base and sides with a double thickness of waxed paper and then lightly grease the paper.

2 ▲ Place all the ingredients in a large mixing bowl.

3 ▲ Stir to combine, then beat thoroughly with a wooden spoon for 3–6 minutes (depending on size), until well mixed.

4 ▲ Spoon the mixture into the prepared pan and smooth the surface with the back of a wet metal spoon. Make a slight impression in the center to help prevent the cake from

5 Bake in the center of the oven. Use the chart opposite as a guide for timing the cake you are baking. Test the cake about 30 minutes before the end of the baking time. If the cake browns too quickly, cover the top loosely with foil. To test if baked, press lightly in the center. If the cake feels firm and when a skewer inserted in the center comes out clean, it is done. Test again at intervals if necessary.

6 Leave the cake to cool in the pan. When completely cool, turn out of the pan. The lining paper can be left on to help keep the cake moist.

RICH FRUIT CAKE CHART

Cake pan sizes	6 in round	7 in round	8 in round	9 in round	10 in round	11 in round	12 in round	13 in round
	5 in square	6 in square	7 in square	8 in square	9 in square	10 in square	11 in square	12 in square
Currants	1¼ cups	1¾ cups	2¼ cups	3 cups	3½ cups	4½ cups	5¼ cups	6 cups
Sultanas	⅔ cup	1 cup	1½ cups	1¾ cups	2 cups	2½ cups	3 cups	3½ cups
Raisins	⅓ cup	⅔ cup	¾ cup	1 cup	1 cup	1⅓ cups	1½ cups	1½ cups
Glacé cherries, halved	¼ cup	⅓ cup	½ cup	½ cup	⅔ cup	¾ cup	1 cup	1¼ cups
Almonds, chopped	⅓ cup	½ cup	¾ cup	1 cup	1¼ cups	1½ cups	1⅔ cups	2 cups
Mixed citrus peel	¼ cup	½ cup	½ cup	⅔ cup	¾ cup	1 cup	1 cup	1⅓ cups
Lemon, grated rind	½	1	1	2	2	2	3	3
Brandy	1½ tbsp	2 tbsp	2½ tbsp	3 tbsp	3½ tbsp	4 tbsp	4½ tbsp	5 tbsp
Flour	1⅓ cups	1¾ cups	2 cups	2¾ cups	3½ cups	4 cups	4½ cups	5½ cups
Ground allspice	1 tsp	1 tsp	1¼ tsp	1½ tsp	1½ tsp	2 tsp	2½ tsp	1 tbsp
Ground nutmeg	¼ tsp	½ tsp	½ tsp	1 tsp	1 tsp	1 tsp	1½ tsp	2 tsp
Ground almonds	½ cup	⅔ cup	¾ cup	1 cup	1¼ cups	1⅓ cups	1½ cups	1⅔ cups
Soft margarine or butter	½ cup	⅔ cup	scant 1 cup	scant 1¼ cups	scant 1½ cups	scant 1¾ cups	scant 2 cups	2¼ cups
Soft brown sugar	⅔ cup	¾ cup	1 cup	1⅓ cups	1½ cups	scant 2 cups	2 cups	2¼ cups
Black molasses	1 tbsp	1 tbsp	1 tbsp	1½ tbsp	2 tbsp	2 tbsp	2 tbsp	2½ tbsp
Eggs, large, beaten	3	4	5	6	7	8	9	10
Approx. baking time	2¼–2½ hours	2½–2¾ hours	3–3½ hours	3¼–3¾ hours	3¾–4¼ hours	4–4½ hours	4½–5¼ hours	5¼–5¾ hours

Light Fruit Cake

For those who prefer a lighter fruit cake, here is a less rich version, still ideal for marzipanning and covering with sugarpaste or royal icing. Follow the ingredients guide in the chart opposite according to the size of cake you wish to make.

3 ▲ Stir to combine, then beat thoroughly with a wooden spoon for 3–4 minutes, depending on the size, until well mixed.

STORING AND FREEZING
When the cake is cold, wrap well in waxed paper, plastic wrap or foil. It will keep for several weeks, stored in an airtight container. As the cake keeps so well, there is no need to freeze, but, if wished, freeze for up to three months.

1 Preheat the oven to 300°F. Grease a deep cake pan, line the sides and base with a double thickness of waxed paper and lightly grease the paper.

2 ▲ Measure and prepare all the ingredients, then place them all together in a large mixing bowl.

4 ▲ Spoon the mixture into the prepared pan and smooth the surface with the back of a wet metal spoon. Make a slight impression in the center to help prevent the cake from doming.

5 Bake in the center of the oven. Use the chart opposite as a guide according to the size of cake you are baking. Test the cake about 15 minutes before the end of the baking time. If the cake browns too quickly, cover the top loosely with foil. To test if baked, press lightly in the center. If the cake feels firm, and when a skewer inserted in the center comes out clean, it is done. Test again at intervals if necessary.

6 Leave the cake to cool in the pan. When completely cool, turn out of the pan. The lining paper can be left on to help keep the cake moist.

Round, square, ring or heart-shaped – the shape of this light fruit cake can be varied to suit the occasion.

LIGHT FRUIT CAKE CHART

Cake pan sizes	6 in round	7 in round	8 in round	9 in round
	5 in square	6 in square	7 in square	8 in square
Soft margarine or butter	½ cup	¾ cup	1 cup	1⅓ cups
Superfine sugar	½ cup	¾ cup	1 cup	1⅓ cups
Orange, grated rind	½	½	1	1
Eggs, large, beaten	3	4	5	6
Flour	1½ cups	1¾ cups	2¾ cups	3½ cups
Baking powder	¼ tsp	½ tsp	½ tsp	1 tsp
Ground allspice	1 tsp	1½ tsp	2 tsp	2½ tsp
Currants	⅓ cup	⅔ cup	1 cup	1½ cups
Sultanas	⅓ cup	⅔ cup	1 cup	1⅓ cups
Raisins	⅓ cup	⅔ cup	1 cup	1⅓ cups
Dried apricots, chopped	7	14	14	21
Mixed cut citrus peel	scant ½ cup	good ½ cup	¾ cup	1 cup
Approx. baking time	2¼ – 2½ hours	2½ – 2¾ hours	2¾ – 3¼ hours	3¼ – 3¾ hours

Truffle Cake Mix

This is a no-cook recipe, using leftover pieces of sponge cake or plain store-bought sponge to make a moist, rich cake mixture, which is used in several of the novelty cakes.

INGREDIENTS
6 oz plain sponge cake pieces
2 cups ground almonds
scant ⅓ cup dark brown sugar, firmly packed
1 tsp ground allspice
pinch of ground cinnamon
finely grated zest of 1 orange
3 tbsp freshly squeezed orange juice
5 tbsp honey

STORING AND FREEZING
The mixture can be made up to two days in advance, wrapped in plastic wrap and stored in an airtight container. Not suitable for freezing.

1 Place the sponge cake pieces into the bowl of a food processor or blender and process for a few seconds to form fine crumbs.

2 Place the cake crumbs, ground almonds, sugar, spices, orange zest, orange juice and honey in a large mixing bowl. Stir well to combine into a thick, smooth mixture.

3 ▲ Use the mixture as directed in the novelty cake recipes. The truffle mixture can be made and molded into any simple shape, such as a log or round balls. The molded mixture can be covered either with marzipan or with sugarpaste icing.

Tip

Dampen your hands slightly before handling the truffle mixture, as it is very sticky.

Here the truffle mixture has been rolled into a log shape to form the sausage in this sweet-tasting novelty Hot Dog cake.

LINING CAKE PANS

Waxed paper is normally used for lining cake pans. The paper lining prevents the cakes from sticking to the pans and makes them easier to turn out. Different cake recipes require slightly different techniques of lining, depending on the shape of the pan, the type of cake mixture, and how long the cake needs to cook. Quick-mix sponge cakes require only one layer of paper to line the base, for example, whereas rich fruit cakes that often bake for several hours if they are large need to be lined with a double layer of paper on the base and sides. This extra protection also helps cakes to cook evenly.

Lining a shallow round pan

This technique is used for a quick-mix sponge cake.

1 Put the pan on a piece of waxed paper and draw around the base of the pan. Cut out the circle just inside the marked line.

2 ▲ Lightly brush the inside of the pan with a little vegetable oil and position the paper circle in the base of the pan. Brush the paper with a little more vegetable oil.

Tip

Softened butter or margarine can be used as a greasing agent in place of vegetable oil, if wished.

Lining a jelly roll pan

1 Put the pan on a piece of waxed paper and draw around the base. Increase the rectangle by 1 inch on all sides. Cut out this rectangle and snip each corner diagonally down to the original rectangle.

2 ▲ Lightly brush the inside of the pan with a little vegetable oil and fit the paper into the pan, overlapping the corners slightly so that they fit neatly. Brush the paper with a little more vegetable oil.

Lining a deep round cake pan

This technique should be used for all rich or light fruit cakes and Madeira cakes. Use this method for a square pan, but cut out the sides separately.

1 Put the pan on a double thickness of waxed paper and draw around the base. Cut out just inside the line.

2 For the sides of the pan, cut out a double thickness strip of waxed paper that will wrap around the outside of the pan, allowing a slight overlap, and which is 1 inch taller than the depth of the pan.

3 Fold over 1 inch along the length of the side lining. Snip the paper along its length, inside the fold, at short, evenly spaced intervals.

4 Brush the inside of the pan with vegetable oil. Slip the side lining into the pan so the snipped edge fits into the curve of the base and sits flat.

5 ▲ Position the base lining in the pan and brush the paper with a little more vegetable oil.

Basic Icing Recipes

Cakes can take on many guises, and nothing enhances their appearance more for that extra special occasion than a little icing. This chapter offers a range of simple classic icing recipes to suit the type of cake you have made and which can be adapted according to the occasion. Ideas range from quick-mix icings, such as butter icing and satin chocolate icing, which may be instantly poured, spread, swirled or piped on to sponge and Madeira cakes or jelly rolls, to the more regal icings, such as royal icing and sugarpaste icing. These are ideal for covering and decorating fruit cakes intended for more formal occasions, such as anniversaries, christenings and weddings.

The icings in this section are all fairly traditional. However, if you want to substitute any of them with a favorite icing recipe when decorating, make sure that it suits the cake on which you are working.

Decorating Equipment

With a few simple tools, it is possible to create the most stunning of cake decorations. Thick swirls of butter icing formed with a spatula, or stark white confectioners' sugar dusted over a contrastingly dark chocolate icing, instantly provide an impressive effect. As your skills develop, however, you will probably want to invest in some specialized pieces of icing equipment, such as those listed here.

Icing Turntable This is one of the most expensive but useful items for either the novice or more advanced cake decorator. Because it revolves, it is particularly handy for piping, or for icing the sides of a round cake with royal icing.
Straight-edge Ruler Choose one made of stainless steel so that it will not bend as you pull it across a layer of royal icing, to give a smooth, flat surface to a cake.
Icing Scrapers These can have straight or serrated edges for giving a smooth or patterned surface to the sides or tops of cakes coated with royal, butter or fudge icing.
Small Rolling Pin Made in a handy size for rolling out small amounts of marzipan or sugarpaste icing for decorations.

Nozzles There are numerous shapes and sizes to choose from, but it is best to start off with some of the basic shapes. Small straight-sided nozzles fit homemade waxed paper piping bags. Larger ones are more suitable for the commercially-made fabric bags when piping large amounts of icing.
Nozzle Brush A small wire brush which makes the job of cleaning out nozzles a lot easier.
Flower Nail Used as a support when piping flowers.
Crimping Tools These are available with different end-shapes which produce varied patterns and offer a quick way of giving a professional finish to a cake.
Paintbrushes Brushes for painting designs on to cakes, adding highlights to flowers or modeled shapes, or for making run-outs are available at cake icing specialists, stationers or art supply shops.
Florists' Wire, Tape and Stamens All available from cake icing specialists. The wire, available in different gauges, is handy for wiring small sugarpaste flowers together to form floral sprays. The tape is used to neaten the stems, and the stamens, available in many colors, form the centers of the flowers.

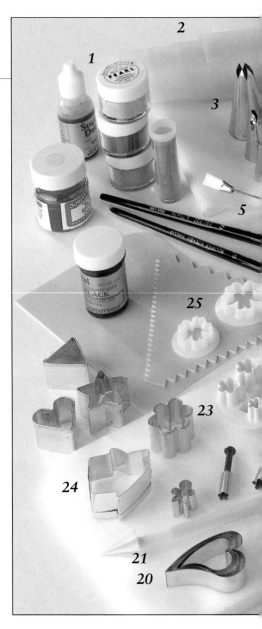

Papers There are two types of papers used in cake decorating. Waxed paper is used for making piping bags and for drying sugar-frosted flowers and fruits, while parchment paper is used for spreading melted chocolate and for icing run-outs.

Cutters Small cocktail cutters are useful for making cut-out shapes from chocolate, sugarpaste and marzipan. Blossom cutters, available in different shapes and sizes, are good for making small flowers, while a special frill cutter can be used to cut out quick-and-easy frills.

1 *food colorings*
2 *waxed paper and parchment paper*
3 *piping nozzles*
4 *fabric piping bag*
5 *nozzle brush*
6 *paintbrushes*
7 *icing turntable*
8 *florists' wire*
9 *stamens*
10 *florists' tape*
11 *straight-edge ruler*
12 *cake pillars*

13 *cake pillar supports*
14 *crimping tools*
15 *food coloring pens*
16 *flower nail*
17 *frill cutter*
18 *textured rolling pin*
19 *foam pad*
20 *shaped cutters*
21 *modeling tool*
22 *plunger cutters*
23 *dual blossom cutter*
24 *cocktail cutters*
25 *plain and serrated side scrapers*

*M*arzipan

With its smooth, pliable texture, marzipan has been popular for centuries in cake making, especially for large cakes such as wedding and christening cakes. It is also excellent for making a variety of cake decorations. The following recipe is sufficient to cover the top and sides of a 7 inch round or a 6 inch square cake. Make half the amount if only the top is to be covered.

INGREDIENTS
Makes 1 lb
2¼ *cups ground almonds*
1 cup confectioners' sugar, sifted
½ *cup superfine sugar*
1 tsp lemon juice
2 drops almond extract
1 medium egg, beaten

STORING
The marzipan will keep for up to four days, wrapped in plastic wrap in an airtight container, and stored in the refrigerator.

1 ▲ Put the ground almonds, confectioners' and superfine sugars into a bowl and mix together.

2 ▲ Add the lemon juice, almond extract and enough beaten egg to mix to a soft but firm dough. Gather together with your fingers to form a ball.

3 ▲ Knead the marzipan on a work surface lightly dusted with sifted confectioners' sugar until smooth.

Using Marzipan

Marzipan is applied to the sides and top of a cake, particularly rich fruit cakes, to prevent moisture seeping through the cake and to provide a smooth undercoat for the top covering of royal icing or sugarpaste icing.

Once the marzipan has been applied, leave it to dry for a day or two before applying the icing. For a richer taste you can mix up your own marzipan. However, if you have any concerns about using raw eggs in uncooked recipes, especially in light of current health warnings, do buy ready-made marzipan. It is very good quality, does not contain raw egg and is available in two colors, white and yellow. White is the best choice if you want to add your own colors and create different molded shapes.

Marzipan can be used as an attractive cake coating in its own right as well as providing a base for other icings.

Sugarpaste Icing

Sugarpaste icing has opened up a whole new concept in cake decorating. It is wonderfully pliable, easy to make and use, and can be colored, molded and shaped in the most imaginative fashion. Though quick to make at home, store-bought sugarpaste, also known as easy-roll or ready-to-roll icing, is very good quality and handy to use. This recipe makes sufficient to cover the top and sides of a 7 inch round or a 6 inch square cake.

INGREDIENTS
Makes 12 oz
1 large egg white
1 tbsp liquid glucose, warmed
3 cups confectioners' sugar, sifted

STORING
The icing will keep for up to a week, wrapped in plastic wrap or a plastic bag and stored in the refrigerator. Bring to room temperature before using. If a thin crust forms, trim off before using or it will make the icing lumpy. Also, if the icing dries out or hardens, knead in a little boiled water to make it smooth and pliable again.

1 Put the egg white and glucose in a bowl. Stir together with a wooden spoon to break up the egg white.

2 ▲ Add the confectioners' sugar and mix together with a spatula or knife, using a chopping action, until well blended and the icing begins to bind together.

3 Knead the mixture with your fingers until it forms a ball.

4 ▲ Knead the sugarpaste on a work surface lightly dusted with sifted confectioners' sugar until smooth, soft and pliable. If the icing is too soft, knead in more sifted confectioners' sugar until it is firm and pliable.

Tip

Ready-made store-bought sugarpaste does not contain raw egg, so do use this if you prefer to avoid uncooked egg in recipes in light of current health warnings.

Tinted or left pure white, sugarpaste icing can be used to cover cakes, and molded to make decorations to suit any shape of cake.

Royal Icing

Royal icing has gained a regal position in the world of icing. Any special occasion cake which demands a classical, professional finish uses this smooth, satin-like icing. The following recipe makes sufficient to cover the top and sides of a 7 inch round or a 6 inch square cake.

INGREDIENTS
Makes 1½ lb
3 large egg whites
about 6 cups confectioners' sugar, sifted
1½ tsp glycerine
few drops lemon juice
food coloring (optional)

STORING
Royal icing will keep for up to three days in an airtight container, stored in the refrigerator. Stir the icing well before using.

Tips

• Always sift confectioners' sugar before using, to get rid of any lumps.
• Never add more than the stated amount of glycerine. Too much will make the icing crumbly and too fragile to use.
• A little lemon juice is added to prevent the icing from discoloring, but too much will make the icing become hard.

1 ▲ Put the egg whites in a bowl and stir lightly with a wooden spoon to break them up.

2 ▲ Add the confectioners' sugar gradually in small quantities, beating well with a wooden spoon between each addition. Add sufficient sugar to make a smooth, white, shiny icing with the consistency of very stiff meringue. It should be thin enough to spread, but thick enough to hold its shape.

3 ▲ Beat in the glycerine, lemon juice and food coloring, if using.

4 It is best to let the icing sit for about 1 hour before using. Cover the surface with a piece of damp plastic wrap or a lid so the icing does not dry out. Before using, stir the icing to burst any air bubbles. Even when working with royal icing, always keep it covered.

Royal Icing Using Pure Albumen Powder

If you are concerned about current health warnings advising against the use of raw eggs in uncooked recipes, try the following recipe.

INGREDIENTS
Makes 1 lb
4 cups confectioners' sugar, sifted
6 tbsp water
7 tsp pure albumen powder

STORING
This royal icing will keep for up to a week in an airtight container, stored in a cool place.

1 Mix the pure albumen powder with the water. Leave to stand for 15 minutes, then stir until the powder dissolves.

2 Sieve the albumen solution into a mixing bowl. Add half the confectioners' sugar and beat until smooth. Add the remaining sugar and beat again for 12–14 minutes or until smooth.

3 Adjust the consistency as needed, adding a little more confectioners' sugar for a stiffer icing or a little water for a thinner one. If storing, transfer to an airtight container, cover the surface of the royal icing with plastic wrap and then close the lid.

ICING CONSISTENCIES

For flat icing

▲ The recipes on the opposite page are for a consistency of icing suitable for flat icing a rich fruit cake covered in marzipan. When the spoon is lifted out of the icing, it should form a sharp point, with a slight curve at the end, known as a "soft peak."

For peaking

▲ Make the royal icing as before, but to a stiffer consistency so that when the spoon is lifted out of the bowl the icing stands in straight peaks.

For piping

For piping purposes, the icing needs to be slightly stiffer than for peaked icing so that it forms a fine, sharp peak when the spoon is lifted out. This allows the icing to flow easily for piping, at the same time enabling it to keep its definition.

For run-outs

For elegant and more elaborate cakes, you may want to pipe outlines of shapes and then fill these in with different colored icing. These are known as run-outs. For the outlines, you need to make the icing to a piping consistency, while for the insides you need a slightly thinner icing with a consistency of thick cream, so that with a little help it will flow within the shapes. Ideally the icing should hold its shape and be slightly rounded after filling the outlines.

The right consistency

If you need to change the consistency of your icing, add a little sifted confectioners' sugar to make it stiffer, or beat in a little egg white for a thinner icing. Be sure to do this carefully, as a little of one or the other will change the consistency quickly.

A traditional look for a classic royal icing. This square rich fruit cake has been marzipanned and then flat iced with three, ultra-smooth layers of royal icing. It is simply, but elegantly, decorated with piped borders, a crisp, white ribbon and fresh roses.

$\mathcal{B}$utter Icing

The creamy, rich flavor and silky smoothness of butter icing are popular with both children and adults. The icing can be varied in color and flavor and makes a decorative filling and coating for sponge and Madeira cakes or jelly rolls. Simply swirled, or more elaborately piped, butter icing gives a delicious and attractive finish. The following quantity makes enough to fill and coat the sides and top of an 8 inch sponge cake.

INGREDIENTS
Makes 12 oz
6 tbsp butter, softened,
or soft margarine
2 cups confectioners' sugar, sifted
1 tsp vanilla extract
2–3 tsp milk

STORING
The icing will keep for up to three days, in an airtight container stored in the refrigerator.

1 ▲ Put the butter or margarine, confectioners' sugar, vanilla extract and 1 tsp of the milk in a bowl.

2 ▲ Beat with a wooden spoon or electric beaters adding sufficient extra milk to give a light, smooth and fluffy consistency.

FLAVORINGS
The following amounts are for a single quantity of icing. Increase or decrease the amounts proportionally as needed.
Chocolate *Blend 1 tbsp cocoa powder with 1 tbsp hot water. Allow to cool before beating into the icing.*
Coffee *Blend 2 tsp instant coffee powder or granules with 1 tbsp boiling water. Allow to cool before beating into the icing.*
Lemon, orange or lime *Substitute the vanilla extract and milk with lemon, orange or lime juice and 2 tsp of finely grated citrus zest. Omit the zest if using the icing for piping. Lightly color the icing with the appropriate shade of food coloring, if wished.*

Generous swirls of butter icing give a mouth-watering effect to a cake.

Glacé Icing

This icing can be made in just a few minutes and can be varied by adding a few drops of food coloring or flavoring. The following quantity makes enough to cover the top and decorate an 8 inch round sponge cake.

INGREDIENTS
Makes 8 oz
2 cups confectioners' sugar
2–3 tbsp warm water or fruit juice
food coloring, optional

STORING
Not suitable for storing. The icing must be used immediately after making.

1 ▲ Sift the confectioners' sugar into a bowl to get rid of any lumps.

2 ▲ Using a wooden spoon, gradually stir in enough water to make an icing with the consistency of thick cream. Beat until the icing is smooth. It should be thick enough to coat the back of the spoon. If it is too runny, beat in a little more sifted confectioners' sugar.

3 To color the icing, beat in a few drops of food coloring. Use the icing immediately for coating or piping.

Drizzled or spread, glacé icing can quickly turn a plain cake into something special.

Fudge Frosting

*A rich, darkly delicious frosting, this can transform a simple sponge cake into
one worthy of a very special occasion. Spread fudge frosting smoothly over the cake or swirl it.
Or be even more elaborate with a little piping - it is very versatile. The following amount
will fill and coat the top and sides of an 8 inch or 9 inch round sponge cake.*

INGREDIENTS
Makes 12 oz
2 x 1 oz squares plain chocolate
2 cups confectioners' sugar, sifted
4 tbsp butter or margarine
3 tbsp milk or light cream
1 tsp vanilla extract

STORING
*Not suitable for storing. The icing
must be used immediately after
making.*

1 ▲ Break the chocolate into small
pieces. Put the chocolate, confectioners' sugar, butter or margarine, milk and
vanilla extract in a heavy-based saucepan.

2 ▲ Stir over a very low heat until the
chocolate and butter or margarine
melt. Remove from the heat and stir
until evenly blended.

3 ▲ Beat the icing frequently as it
cools until it thickens sufficiently
to use for spreading or piping. Use
immediately and work quickly once it
has reached the right consistency.

*Thick glossy swirls of fudge icing
almost make a decoration in
themselves on this cake.*

Satin Chocolate Icing

Shiny as satin and smooth as silk, this dark chocolate icing can be poured over a sponge cake. A few fresh flowers, pieces of fresh fruit, simple chocolate shapes or white chocolate piping add the finishing touch. Use this recipe to cover an 8 inch square or a 9 inch round quick-mix sponge or Madeira cake.

INGREDIENTS
Makes 8 oz
6 x 1oz squares plain chocolate
⅔ cup light cream
½ tsp instant coffee powder

STORING
Not suitable for storing. The icing must be used immediately after making.

Tip

Before using the icing, place the cake on a wire rack positioned over a baking sheet or a piece of waxed paper. This will avoid unnecessary mess on the work surface.

2 ▲ Stir over a very low heat until the chocolate melts and the mixture is smooth and evenly blended.

3 Remove from the heat and then immediately pour the icing over the cake, letting it slowly run down the sides to coat it completely. Spread the icing with a spatula as necessary, working quickly before the icing has time to thicken.

Satin chocolate icing brings a real touch of sophistication to the most humble of cakes.

1 ▲ Break the chocolate into small pieces. Put the chocolate, cream and coffee in a small heavy-based saucepan. Place the cake to be iced on a wire rack.

overing Cakes

Covering cakes with icing – whether marzipan, royal or sugarpaste – not only provides a wonderful surface for decorating but also helps to keep the cakes moist. The icings need to be applied with care to ensure that the finish is beautifully smooth. Always plan ahead; it will take several days to marzipan and royal ice a cake, allowing for the drying out times.

Marzipanning a Cake for Sugarpaste Icing

Marzipan can be applied as an icing in its own right, but is mainly used as a base for sugarpaste or royal icing. Unlike a cake covered in royal icing which traditionally has sharp, well defined corners, a cake covered in sugarpaste has much smoother lines with rounded corners and edges. There are therefore two different techniques depending on how you wish to ice the cake.

1 If the cake is not absolutely flat, fill any hollows or build up the top edge (if it is lower than the top of the cake) with a little marzipan. Brush the top of the cake with a little warmed and sieved apricot jam.

2 ▲ Lightly dust a work surface with confectioners' sugar. Knead the marzipan into a smooth ball. Roll out to a ¼ inch thickness and large enough to cover the top and sides of the cake, allowing about an extra 3 inches all around for trimming. Make sure the marzipan does not stick to the work surface and moves freely.

3 ▲ Lift the marzipan using your hands, or place it over a rolling pin to support it, and position over the top of the cake. Drape the marzipan over the cake to cover it evenly.

4 ▲ Smooth the top with the palm of your hand to eliminate any air bubbles. Then carefully lift up the edges of the marzipan and let them fall against the sides of the cake, being careful not to stretch the marzipan. Ensure the marzipanned sides are flat and there are no creases - all the excess marzipan should fall on to the work surface. Use the palms of your hands to smooth the sides and eliminate air bubbles.

5 ▲ With a sharp knife, trim the excess marzipan, cutting it flush with the base of the cake.

6 ▲ With your hands, work in a circular motion over the surface of the marzipan to give it a smooth finish. Spread a little royal icing over the middle of a cake board and place the cake in the center to secure. Lay a piece of waxed paper over the top to protect the surface, then leave the cake for at least 12 hours to dry before covering with icing.

Marzipanning a Round Cake for Royal Icing

1 ▲ If the cake is not absolutely flat, fill any hollows or build up the top edge (if it is lower than the top of the cake) with a little marzipan.

2 Brush the top of the cake with warmed and sieved apricot jam.

3 Lightly dust a work surface with confectioners' sugar. Using one-third of the marzipan, knead it into a ball. Roll out to a round ¼ inch thickness and ½ inch larger than the top of the cake. Make sure that the marzipan does not stick to the work surface and moves freely.

4 ▲ Invert the top of the cake on to the marzipan. Trim the marzipan almost to the edge of the cake. With a small metal spatula, press the marzipan inwards so it is flush with the edge of the cake.

▶ The method for marzipanning a square cake for royal icing is the same as for a round one, except for the sides. Measure the length and height of the sides with string and roll out the marzipan in four separate pieces, using the string measurements as a guide.

5 Carefully turn the cake the right way up. Check the sides of the cake. If there are any holes, fill them with marzipan to make a flat surface. Brush the sides with apricot jam.

6 Knead the remaining marzipan and any trimmings (making sure there are no cake crumbs on the work surface) to form a ball. For the sides of the cake, measure the circumference with a piece of string, and the height of the sides with another piece.

7 ▲ Roll out a strip of marzipan to the same thickness as the top, matching the length and width to the measured string. Hold the cake on its side, being careful to touch the marzipanned top as lightly as possible. Roll the cake along the marzipan strip, pressing the marzipan into position to cover the sides. Trim if necessary to fit.

8 ▲ Smooth the joins together with a spatula. Spread a little royal icing into the middle of a cake board and place the cake in the center to secure. Lay a piece of waxed paper very loosely over the top to protect the surface, then leave for at least 24 hours to dry before covering with icing.

Tip

When buying marzipan, it is best to choose the white kind for covering a cake, as the bright yellow marzipan may discolor pale colored sugarpaste or royal icing.

Covering a Round Cake with Royal Icing

A cake which is coated with royal icing is always covered with marzipan first. The marzipan should be applied one to two days before the royal icing so it has time to dry out slightly, giving a firm surface on which to work. The royal icing is then built up in two or three layers, each one being allowed to dry out before covering with the next. The final coat should be perfectly flat and smooth, with no air bubbles.

Tip

It is difficult to calculate the exact amount of icing required, but if you work with 1 lb/⅔ quantity batches, it should always be fresh. While working, keep the royal icing in a bowl and cover tightly with a clean, damp cloth or plastic wrap so it does not dry out.

1 The icing should be of "soft peak" consistency. Put about 2 tbsp of icing in the center of the marzipanned cake (the exact amount will depend on the size of cake you are icing).

2 ▲ Using a small spatula, spread the icing over the top of the cake, working back and forth with the flat of the blade to eliminate any air bubbles. Keep working the icing in this way until the top of the cake is completely covered. Carefully trim any icing that extends over the edge of the cake with the spatula.

3 ▲ Position a straight-edge ruler on the top edge of the cake furthest away from you. Slowly and smoothly pull the ruler across the surface of the icing, holding it at a slight angle. Do this without stopping to prevent ridges forming. You may need several attempts to get a smooth layer, in which case simply re-spread the top of the cake with icing and try again.

4 ▲ Trim any excess icing from the top edges of the cake with the spatula to give a straight, neat edge. Leave the icing to dry for several hours, or preferably overnight, in a dry place before continuing.

5 ▲ Place the cake on a turntable. To cover the sides, spread some icing on to the side of the cake with a spatula. Rock the spatula back and forth as you spread the icing to eliminate air bubbles. Rotate the turntable as you work your way around the cake.

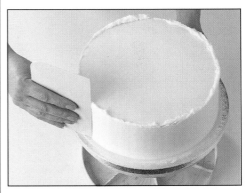

6 ▲ Using a plain side-scraper, hold it firmly in one hand against the side of the cake at a slight angle. Turn the turntable round in a continuous motion and in one direction with the other hand, while pulling the scraper smoothly in the opposite direction to give a smooth surface to the iced sides. When you have completed the full turn, carefully lift off the scraper to leave a neat join. Trim off any excess icing from the top edge and the cake board.

7 Leave the cake to dry, uncovered, then apply the icing in the same way to give the cake two or three more coats of icing. For a really smooth final layer, use a slightly softer consistency of icing.

Covering a Square Cake Rough Icing a Cake

The method is essentially the same as for icing a round cake.

1 Cover the top with icing as for the round cake. Leave to dry.

2 ▲ Cover the sides as for the round cake, but work on one side at a time and allow the icing to dry out before continuing with the next side. You will not need a turntable. Simply pull the scraper firmly and smoothly across each side in a single movement, repeating if necessary, for a really smooth finish.

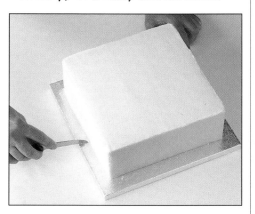

3 ▲ Trim off any excess icing from the cake board with a knife.

4 Leave the cake to dry, uncovered, then apply the icing in the same way to give the cake two or three more coats of icing. For a really smooth final layer, use a slightly softer consistency.

This colorful Christmas Tree cake shows an interesting version of peaked, or rough, icing. The fruit cake is first covered with colored marzipan and left to dry for 12 hours, then royal icing is peaked around the lower half of the sides. The decorations are also made of colored marzipan.

Peaking the icing to give it a rough appearance, like that of snow, is a much quicker and simpler way of applying royal icing to a cake. It is also much quicker to apply as you only need one covering of icing.

1 ▲ Spread the icing evenly over the cake, bringing the icing right to the edges so the cake is completely covered.

2 ▲ Starting at the bottom of the cake, press the flat side of a spatula into the icing, then pull away sharply to form a peak. Repeat until the whole cake is covered with icing peaks. Alternatively, flat ice the top of the cake and rough ice the sides – or vice versa.

Covering with Sugarpaste Icing

Sugarpaste icing is a quick, professional way to cover a cake. Although fruit cakes are usually covered with marzipan first, this is not necessary if you are using a sponge base. The sugarpaste can be applied in one coating, unlike royal icing which requires several coats for a really smooth finish. Keep the icing white or knead in a little food coloring to tint. Ready-made sugarpaste is extremely good quality and is available in various colors for fast and professional results.

1 Carefully brush a little water or sherry over the marzipanned surface to help the icing stick to the marzipan. (If you miss a patch, unsightly air bubbles may form.)

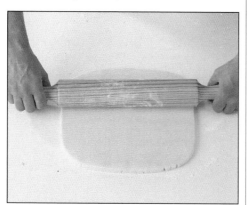

2 ▲ Lightly dust a work surface with confectioners' sugar. Roll out the sugarpaste to a ¼ inch thickness and large enough to cover the top and sides of the cake plus a little extra for trimming. Make sure the icing does not stick to the surface and moves freely.

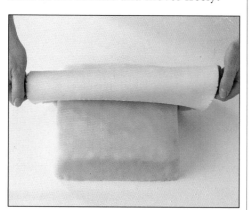

3 ▲ Lift the sugarpaste using your hands, or place it over a rolling pin to support it, and position over the top of the cake. Drape the sugarpaste over the cake to cover it evenly.

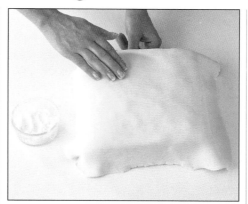

4 ▲ Dust your hands with a little cornstarch. Smooth the top and sides of the cake with your hands, working from top to bottom, to eliminate any air bubbles.

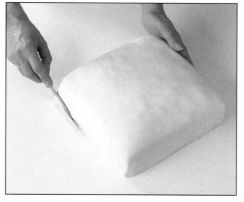

5 ▲ With a sharp knife, trim off the excess sugarpaste, cutting flush with the base of the cake.

6 Spread a little royal icing into the middle of a cake board and place the cake in the center to secure.

Tip

To avoid damaging the surface of the cake while you move it, slide the cake to the edge of the work surface and support it underneath with your hand. Lift it and place on the cake board.

Covering Awkward Shapes

Although most shapes of cake can be covered smoothly with one piece of sugarpaste icing, there are some which need to be covered in sections. A cake baked in a ring mold is one example. The top and outer side of the cake are covered with two identical pieces of sugarpaste, and the inner side with a third piece.

1 ▲ Measure half of the outer circumference of the cake with a piece of string, then measure the side and rounded top with another piece of string.

2 ▲ Take three-quarters of the sugarpaste icing and cut in half. Keep the remaining icing well wrapped until needed. Brush the marzipan lightly with water. Roll out each half of the icing into a rectangle, matching the string measurements. Cover the top and side of the cake in two halves.

3 Measure the circumference and the height of the inner side with two pieces of string. Roll out the reserved sugarpaste icing into a rectangle matching the string measurements, and use to cover the inside of the ring. Trim the sugarpaste to fit and press the joins together securely.

FOOD COLORINGS & TINTS

Food colorings and tints for cake making are available today in almost as large a range as those found on an artist's palette. This has opened up endless possibilities for the cake decorator to create the most imaginative and colorful designs. Liquid colors are only suitable for marzipan and sugarpaste icing if a few drops are required to tint the icing a very pale shade. If used in large amounts they will soften the icings too much. So for vibrant, stronger colors, as well as for subtle sparkling tints, use pastes or powders, available from cake icing specialists. When choosing colors for icings, ensure that they are harmonious, and complement your design.

Coloring icings

How you apply the color to an icing depends on whether it is in liquid form, a paste or powder. While working with the colorings it is best to stand them on a plate or washable board so they do not mark your work surface. When using toothpicks for transferring the color to the icing, select a fresh stick for each color so the colors do not become mixed together.

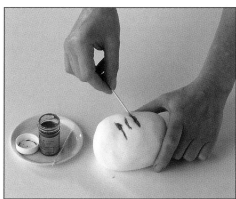

2 ▲ To color firmer icings, such as sugarpaste and marzipan, use paste colorings. Dip a toothpick into the coloring and streak it on to the surface of a ball of the icing.

4 ▲ To create subtle pants in specific areas, brush powdered colorings on to the surface of the icing.

1 ▲ Add liquid color to the icing a few drops at a time until the required shade is reached. Stir into softer icings, such as butter, royal or glacé.

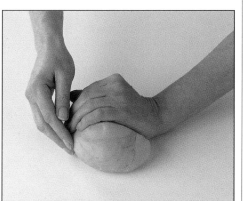

3 ▲ Knead thoroughly until the color is evenly worked in and there is no streaking. Add sparingly at first, remembering that the color becomes more intense as the icing stands, then leave for about 10 minutes to see if it is the shade you need.

A cake decorator's palette – a vivid array of food colorings to help bring out the artist in you.

ecorating with Royal Icing

Of all the icings, royal icing is probably the most complex and hardest to work with. But once the techniques are mastered, it provides a classic backdrop for both traditional as well as more contemporary cake designs. Traditionally it is used for decorating white wedding and Christmas cakes, but, as color is being introduced more and more into cake decorating, royal icing can now be used in many imaginative ways. This chapter demonstrates how to introduce a modern look using a wide variety of classic techniques.

Making and Using Piping Bags

A piping bag is an essential tool when working with royal icing. You can buy piping bags made of washable fabric and icing syringes, which are ideal for the beginner or for piping butter icing in bold designs. However, for more intricate piping, particularly if using several icing colors and nozzles, homemade waxed paper or parchment paper piping bags are more practical and flexible to handle. Make up several ahead of time, following the instructions given here, then fit them with straight-sided nozzles. Do not use nozzles with ridges as they do not have such a tight fit in the bag. To prevent the icing drying out when working with several bags, cover the nozzle ends with a damp cloth when they are not in use.

2 ▶ With the point of the triangle facing away from you, hold the triangle with your thumb in the middle of the longest edge. Take the left corner and bring it over to meet the point of the triangle, as shown.

3 ▼ Hold in position and bring the remaining corner round and back over to meet the other two points, forming a cone shape. Holding all the points together, position them to make the cone tight and the point of it sharp, as shown.

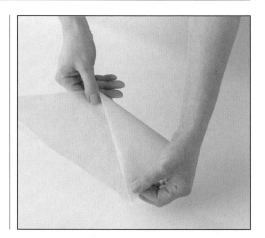

1 ▲ Cut out a 10 inch square of waxed paper or parchment paper, then fold this in half diagonally to make a triangle.

4 ▲ With the cone open, turn the points neatly inside the top edge, creasing firmly down. Secure the cone with a staple.

5 For using with a nozzle, cut off the pointed end of the bag and position the nozzle so it fits snugly into the point. Half-fill the bag with icing and fold over the top to seal. To use without a nozzle, add the icing, seal, then cut a small straight piece off the end of the bag to pipe lines.

6 For ease and control, it is important to hold the bag in a relaxed position. You may find it easier to hold it with one or both hands. For one hand, hold the bag between your middle and index fingers and push out the icing with your thumb.

7 ▲ If using both hands, simply wrap the other hand around the bag in the same manner, so both thumbs can push the icing out.

8 ▲ To pipe, hold the bag so the nozzle is directly over the area you want to pipe on. The bag will be held straight or at an angle, depending on the shape you are piping. Gently press down with your thumb on the top of the bag to release the icing, and lift your thumb to stop the flow of icing. Use a small spatula to cut off any excess icing from the tip of the nozzle as you lift the bag from each piped shape, to keep the shapes neat.

Royal icing is the perfect icing for piping. This cake shows how you can achieve pretty effects with shells, stars, lines and beads. Piped roses in full bloom complement the color chosen for the top of the cake, and the petal tips have been highlighted with food coloring. Carry the design on to the cake board for a classic celebratory cake.

Piping Shapes

Royal icing gives cakes a professional finish, and is often used in decorating to give a formal and ornate character to a cake. However, simple piping skills can easily be achieved given a little practice. This section shows you how, with just a few piping nozzles, you can enhance the look of your cakes. Remember that the icing must be of the correct consistency – not too firm or it will be difficult to squeeze out of the piping bag, and not too soft or the piping will not hold its shape. Small nozzles are used for the delicate designs made with royal icing. Larger ones are more suitable for butter icing and frostings.

Stars, swirls and scrolls

PIPING TWISTED ROPES AND LEAVES

For the ropes, fit nozzles Nos 43 or 44, or a writing nozzle, into a waxed paper piping bag and half-fill with icing. Hold the bag at a slight angle and pipe in a continuous line with even pressure, twisting the bag as you pipe. For leaves, you can use a No 18 petal nozzle or simply cut off the point of the bag in the shape of an arrow. Place the tip of the bag on the cake, holding the bag at a slight angle. Pipe out the icing, then pull away quickly to make the tapering end of a leaf.

Twisted ropes and leaves

PIPING STARS

For a simple star shape, choose a star-shaped nozzle in a size to suit your design. Hold the piping bag upright directly over the area to be iced. Gently squeeze the bag to release the icing and to form a star. Pull off quickly and sharply, keeping the bag straight, to give a neat point to the star.

PIPING SWIRLS

Choose a star-shaped nozzle in a size to suit your design. Hold the piping bag directly over the area to be iced. Pipe a swirl in a circular movement, then pull off quickly and sharply, keeping the bag straight to leave a neat point.

PIPING SCROLLS

Choose star or rope nozzles in a size to suit your design. Hold the piping bag at a slight angle and place the tip of the nozzle on the cake. Pipe the icing lightly upwards and outwards, then come down in a circular movement, tailing off the icing so the end rests on the cake to make a scroll. The action is a little like piping a large "comma." For a reverse scroll, repeat as before, but pipe in the opposite direction, going inwards to reverse the shape. A scroll border can be particularly effective if you alternate two colors of icing.

PIPING CORNELLI

Cornelli is a fun technique which can be carried out in one or more colors. It is a little like doodling. Use writing nozzles Nos 1 or 2 and pipe a continuous flow of icing, squiggling the lines in the shape of W's and M's.

PIPING SIMPLE EMBROIDERY

Piped embroidery is very fine work, requiring writing nozzles Nos 0 or 1. Keep the design simple and work in one or several colors. Pipe little circles, lines and dots to make a delicate pattern for your cake. Look at textile embroidery designs for some ideas.

Cornelli and simple embroidery

PIPING DOTS OR BEADS

Use writing nozzles Nos 1, 2 or 3. Hold the piping bag directly over the area you wish to pipe. Press out the icing so it forms a bead, then release the pressure on the bag and take it off gently to one side. The smaller size nozzle will make simple dots. Neither dots nor beads should end in a sharp point. If this happens, lightly press any sharp points back into the bead with a small damp brush, or try making the icing a little softer.

PIPING SHELLS

Use star nozzles Nos 5 or 8. Rest the tip of the nozzle on the cake and pipe out a little icing to secure it to the surface. Gently squeeze out the icing while lifting the bag slightly up and then down, ending with the nozzle back on the surface of the cake. Pull off to release the icing. Repeat, allowing the beginning of the next shell to touch the end of the first one and carry on in this way until you have completed a continuous line of shells.

PIPING LINES

Use a writing nozzle, remembering that the smaller the hole, the finer the line. Hold the bag at an angle, rest the nozzle on the cake and pipe out a little icing to secure it to the surface. Pipe the icing, lifting the bag slightly as you work, so it is just above the surface of the cake. Continue to pipe, allowing the line of piping to fall in a straight line. Do not pull or the line will break. At the end of the line, release the pressure, rest the nozzle on the surface of the cake and pull off to break the icing. The line can be varied by curving or looping it.

PIPING TRELLISES

To pipe trellises, use the same technique as above to pipe a set of parallel lines. Then overpipe a set in the opposite direction for squares, or horizontally across the lines for diamonds. You can also get different effects by using different widths of writing nozzles.

PIPING ZIGZAGS

Use a No 2 or 3 writing nozzle and pipe either one continuous zigzag, or stop and start at the end of each point to make them sharper.

Dots and beads

Shells

Lines, trellises and zigzags

Piped Sugar Pieces

These little piped sugar pieces are very fragile and have the appearance of fine lace. They must be made ahead of time, and left to dry. The sugar pieces need to be handled carefully, and it is a good idea to make plenty in case of breakages.

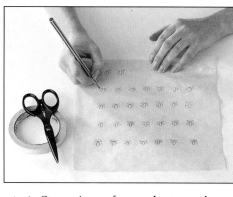

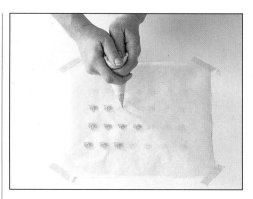

1 ▲ On a piece of waxed paper, draw your chosen design several times with pencil. The designs should be kept fairly small.

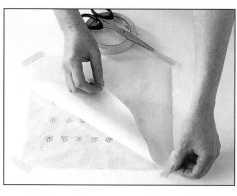

Shapely forms – delicate piped sugar pieces can be made in all kinds of designs and colors and attached to the sides, tops or edges of cakes with a dab of royal icing.

2 ▲ Tape the paper to the work surface or a flat board and secure a piece of waxed paper or parchment paper over the top. Tape the paper down at the corners with masking tape.

3 ▲ Fit a piping bag with a No 1 writing nozzle. Half-fill with royal icing, and fold over the top to seal. Pipe over each design, carefully following the penciled lines with a continuous thread of icing. Repeat, piping as many pieces as you need plus a few extra in case of any breakages.

4 Leave to dry for at least two hours. Remove from the paper by carefully turning it back and lifting off each piece with a spatula. When dry, store in a box between layers of tissue paper.

Simple Piped Flowers

To make these pretty piped flowers, you will need a petal nozzle – either small, medium or large depending on how big you want the flowers to be – a paper piping bag, a toothpick and a flower nail. Make the flowers ahead of time and, when dry, store in a box between layers of tissue paper.

ROSE

1 For a tightly formed rose, make a fairly firm icing. Color the icing, or leave it white. Fit the petal nozzle into a paper piping bag, half-fill with royal icing and fold over the top to seal.

2 Hold the piping bag so the wider end of the nozzle is pointing into what will be the base of the flower, and hold a toothpick in the other hand. Carefully pipe a small cone shape around the tip of a toothpick. Pipe a petal half way around the cone, lifting it so that it is at an angle and curling outwards, not flat, and turning the toothpick at the same time.

3 ▲ Repeat with more petals so they overlap each other slightly. The last petals can lie flatter and be more open. Remove the rose from the toothpick by threading the toothpick through a large hole on a grater. The rose will rest on the grater. Leave until dry and firm.

PANSY

1 Color the icing. Fit the petal nozzle into a paper piping bag, half-fill with royal icing and fold over the top to seal. Cut out a small square of waxed paper and secure to the flower nail with a little icing.

2 ▲ Holding the nozzle flat, pipe the petal shape in a curve, turning the flower nail at the same time. Pipe five petals in all. Pipe beads of yellow icing in the center with a small writing nozzle, or use florists' stamens.

3 Remove the paper from the flower nail, but leave the pansy on the paper until it is dry and firm. Colored details can be added by painting with food coloring, or using food coloring pens, once the flower has dried. Lift the pansy from the paper by carefully slipping a spatula underneath the base of the flower.

COLORED SUMMER FLOWERS

1 Color the icing. Make up the flowers in a variety of shades for a colorful arrangement. Fit the petal nozzle into a paper piping bag, half-fill with royal icing and fold over the top to seal. Cut out a small square of waxed paper and secure to the flower nail with a little icing.

2 ▲ Pipe five flat petals in a circle so they slightly overlap each other. Pipe beads of yellow icing in the center of each flower or sprinkle with hundreds and thousands. Leave to dry and add colored details as for the pansy.

Bouquet of iced blossoms, including roses, pansies and bright summer flowers – arrangements of piped flowers make colorful cake decorations.

Run-outs

Designs for run-outs can be as complicated or as simple as you like. It is best to start off with a fairly solid shape for your first attempt, as these decorations can be quite fragile to handle. Always make a few more run-outs than you think you will need in case of breakages.

1 Make up the royal icings to the correct consistencies: a stiffer one for the outline, and a softer one for filling in (see the basic recipe for Royal Icing). Leave the icing to stand, preferably overnight, to allow any air bubbles to come to the surface. Stir the icing before using. On a piece of waxed paper, draw your chosen design several times.

2 ▲ Tape the paper to the work surface or a flat board and lay a piece of parchment paper over the top. Tape the paper down at the corners with masking tape.

3 ▲ Fit a paper piping bag with a No 1 writing nozzle, and half-fill with the stiffer icing for piping the outline. Carefully pipe over the outline of your design with a continuous thread of icing.

4 ▲ Add the softer icing for filling in into a second paper piping bag. Cut the pointed end off the bag in a straight line. Do not make it too big, or the icing will flow out too quickly. Pipe the icing into the outlines to fill, working from the outline into the center, being careful not to touch the outline or it may break. To prevent air bubbles forming, keep the end of the bag in the icing. The icing should look overfilled and rounded, as it will shrink slightly as it dries.

5 ▲ You now need to work quickly while the icing is still soft. Move a paintbrush carefully through the icing to fill in any gaps and to ensure it goes right to the edge of the outline, keeping the icing smooth. If any air bubbles do appear, smooth them out with the brush or burst with a pin.

6 ▲ Leave the run-outs on the paper to dry; the drying time will vary depending on their size, but leave for at least one day and preferably longer. When completely dry, remove by carefully slipping a spatula under the shapes and easing them off the paper. Decorative details can then be piped on to the dried run-outs. Allow these to dry before using or storing.

7 Store the run-outs in a box between layers of waxed paper.

When royal icing is presented in bright colors it takes on a lively new look. The hearts and brilliant butterflies are made using the run-out technique. The wings are made separately, then joined with a line of piping to form the body of each butterfly. This also secures them to the cake. Piped sugar pieces, scroll borders and polka dots complete the design.

ecorating with Sugarpaste Icing

As a covering, sugarpaste icing gives a softer look to a cake than royal icing. It is much quicker to work with, requiring only one rolled out layer. This is then placed in position so it curves itself over the edges of the cake. Because it is so pliable, sugarpaste can also be used for a wide range of decorative effects. When making sugarpaste decorations, always wrap any icing you are not using immediately in plastic wrap to stop it drying out.

Marbling

As an alternative to covering a cake in a single color, sugarpaste icing can be marbled for a multi-colored effect. Use several colors and keep them quite vibrant, or use one or two delicate tones. Marbled sugarpaste icing can also be used to make effective molded flowers and other modeled decorations.

1 ▲ Form the sugarpaste icing into a smooth roll or ball. Dip the end of a toothpick into the food coloring and dab a few drops on to the icing. Repeat with more colors if wished.

2 ▲ Knead the sugarpaste icing just a few times. The coloring should look very patchy.

3 ▲ On a work surface lightly sprinkled with confectioners' sugar, roll out the sugarpaste icing to reveal the marbled effect.

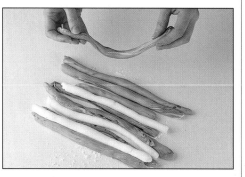

4 ▲ Alternatively, for a very bold interweaving of colors, use the following technique. Divide the sugarpaste icing into three or four equal portions, depending on how many colors you want to use. Color with food coloring. Divide each color into four or five portions and roll out with your hands into sausage shapes. You could even put two colors together for an instant marbled sausage. Place the different-colored sausages side-by-side on the work surface.

5 ▲ Twist the colors together and knead for several seconds until the strips of color are fused together but retain their individual colors.

6 ▲ Roll out the marbled icing on a work surface lightly dusted with confectioners' sugar.

Crimping

Crimping tools are similar to large tweezers with patterned ends and are available in a good variety of styles. Crimping is a very quick and efficient way of giving decorative edges and borders to sugarpaste-coated cakes – the effect is similar to the embroidery technique of smocking. For a simple finish to the crimped cake, top with a small posy of edible flowers, a ribbon, or other bought decorations.

1 ▲ Cover the cake with sugarpaste icing. For crimping, the icing must still be soft, so do not allow it to dry out before decorating. Dip the crimping tool in a little cornstarch.

2 ▼ Position the crimping tool on the cake in the place you wish to start the design and squeeze the teeth together to make the pattern.

3 ▲ Slowly release the crimper so as not to tear the icing. Repeat the pattern, either touching the last one or spacing them evenly apart. The pattern can be varied by using different crimping tools.

4 ▲ The same technique can be used to crimp decorative designs down the sides of a cake. If applying sugarpaste frills to a cake, crimp the edges for a neat and pretty finish.

Embossing

Special embossing tools can be purchased from cake icing specialists, but you can also use any other patterned items such as cookie cutters or piping nozzles.

1 ▲ Cover the cake with sugarpaste icing. For embossing, the icing must still be soft, so do not allow it to dry out. Brush a little cornstarch on to the embossing tool and press firmly on to the soft icing. Repeat, brushing with cornstarch each time.

2 ▲ To add color, brush a little powdered food coloring on to the embossing tool instead of the cornstarch and press on to the icing as before. Highlights can also be added with food coloring pens, as shown.

3 ▲ Textured rolling pins are also available from cake icing specialists. Cover the cake with sugarpaste icing as before and smooth over with your hand. Roll over the surface of the icing with the textured rolling pin. This rolling pin gives a basketweave effect.

Modeling

Sugarpaste is wonderfully adaptable, and can be used to model almost any shape you can think of. Choose small objects, such as flowers, fruits, vegetables, animals, or whatever is going to suit your cake. Using this technique, every cake you make will be unique. Remember to dust the work surface lightly with confectioners' sugar before you start, to prevent sticking. Leave the modeled shapes to dry on waxed paper, before applying to the cake.

SMART TEDDY BEAR

▲ Mold each part of the bear's body separately in cream-colored sugarpaste icing. Roll out the waistcoat to fit the body and cut out the bow tie in purple icing. Mold the buttons and eyes in black icing. Attach the head to the body with a little water, pressing together to secure. Brush the body lightly with water and wrap the waistcoat round, folding back the top two corners. Attach the arms, legs and ears with a little water, pressing to secure, then bend into shape. Attach the bow tie, buttons and eyes with a little water, then paint on any details such as nose and mouth with brown food coloring.

FROSTY SNOWMAN

▲ Mold the snowman's body, head and arms in white sugarpaste icing. Roll out the scarf in red icing, cutting the ends with a sharp knife to represent the tassels. Shape two small balls of blue icing for the eyes, one of red for the nose and two of black for buttons. Using black icing, shape the hat in two pieces, as shown. Attach the head to the body with a little water, then the arms, pressing lightly to secure. Attach the scarf, eyes, nose, buttons and hat in the same way.

HUNGRY RABBIT

▼ Mold the rabbit's body and head, legs, tail and ears in light brown sugarpaste icing. Shape two small balls of blue icing for the eyes. Attach the tail, legs and ears to the rabbit's body with a little water, pressing lightly to secure. Paint the nose and details on the eyes with brown food coloring. For the carrots, shape long ovals out of orange icing, tapering at one end, then make markings on them with the back of a knife. Attach small pieces of green icing on to the ends.

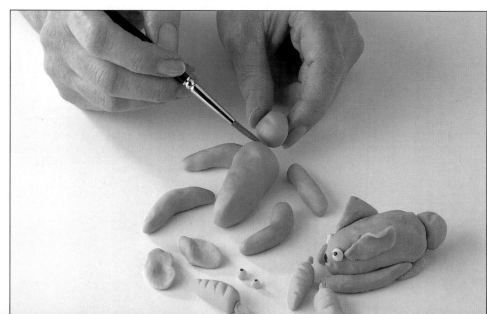

CAT ON A MAT

▲ Mold and shape the cat's body, head, legs, tail and ears in gray marbled sugarpaste icing. Shape two small ovals in black for the eyes and a small pink ball for the nose. Roll out a piece of green icing for the mat. Attach the head to the body with a little water, then the legs, tail, ears, eyes and nose, pressing lightly to secure and bending into shape where necessary. Press four short lengths of florists' wire into the head to represent whiskers (these must be removed before serving the cake). Paint the mouth with black food coloring and place the cat on the mat.

Let your imagination run riot when it comes to using sugarpaste icing. All the inhabitants of this water-lily pond are molded or cut out of sugarpaste. The water lilies are formed with a small petal-shaped cocktail cutter, then bent into shape. The lily pads are formed with a small round cutter, and then snipped with a knife to make them more lifelike. A blossom cutter creates the flowers on the grassy bank, and the irises, bulrushes, frog and goldfish are modeled by hand.

Cut-out Shapes

Using a variety of shaped cutters, sugarpaste icing can be stamped out to make all kinds of colorful shapes for decorating cakes.

1 Color the sugarpaste icing to the desired shade, then roll out evenly on a work surface lightly dusted with confectioners' sugar.

2 ▲ Dip the ends of the cutter in cornstarch and cut out the shapes. Leave to dry flat on waxed paper, then attach the shapes to the cake with a little royal icing.

The sky's the limit – use cutters or make your own templates for creating a variety of cut-out images.

Cut-out Borders

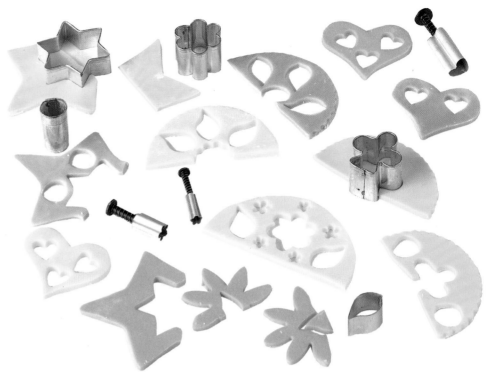

Borders on the cutting edge – cut-out shapes can also be positioned around the edge of a cake to add a decorative border. Make the borders in bold or delicate designs so that they fit the character of the cake.

1 ▲ Roll out the sugarpaste icing thinly and cut out with a medium-sized cutter - a round, fluted cookie cutter has been used here. Leave whole or cut in half, depending on the shape.

2 ▲ Use smaller cutters to cut out inside shapes for a filigree effect, or make up your own shapes and use templates cut out of card.

3 Leave the shapes to dry flat on waxed paper, then attach them around the top edges of the cake with a little royal icing.

Plunger Blossoms

A special plunger blossom cutter, available in different sizes, is used to make these dainty flowers. The cutter contains a plunger for ejecting the delicate shapes once they have been cut out.

1 ▲ Roll out the icing thinly on a work surface lightly dusted with confectioners' sugar. Dip the cutter in cornstarch and cut out the flower shapes.

2 ▲ The flower should remain on the end of the cutter. To remove the flower, hold the cutter on a foam pad and depress the plunger. As it goes into the foam it will bend the flower into shape and release it.

3 The flowers can be simply finished with a little bead of royal icing piped into the center when they are dry, or you can make a spray of flowers using florists' wire and stamens.

4 ▲ To make a spray, push a pin through the center of each flower. Leave the flowers to dry on the foam.

5 ▲ When dry, pipe a little royal icing on to a stamen and thread it through the hole. This will hold it in position. Repeat with all the flowers.

6 ▲ When the individual flowers are completely dry, twist a piece of florists' wire on to the end of each stamen. Group the flowers and twist the wires together to make a spray.

This pretty Teddy Bear Christening cake is simply decorated with a modeled bear and some delicate plunger blossoms.

Frills

Sugarpaste frills give a particularly elaborate finish to a cake and are especially appropriate for decorating wedding, christening and anniversary cakes. Try layering two different colored frills together for a very special occasion.

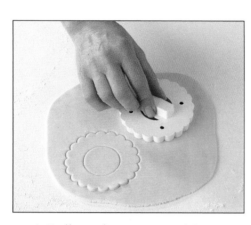

1 ▲ Roll out the sugarpaste icing thinly on a work surface lightly dusted with confectioners' sugar. Use a special frill cutter to cut out the rings for the frills. One ring will make one large or two smaller frills.

2 ▲ Position the end of a wooden toothpick over about ¼ inch of the outer edge of the ring. Roll the toothpick back and forth firmly around the edge with your finger. The edge will become thinner and start to frill. Continue in this way until the ring is completely frilled.

3 ▲ Using a sharp knife, cut through the ring once to open it up. Gently ease it open. For shorter frills, cut the ring in half to make two frills.

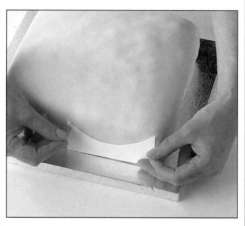

4 ▲ Cut out a template the size of the opened frill and hold against the side of a covered cake. Mark with a pin to show where to attach the frill, and repeat all around the cake.

5 ▲ To attach the frill, either pipe a line of royal icing on to the cake or brush a line of water. Carefully secure the frill on to the line of royal icing or water. Overlay with a second frill in the same or a different colored icing if wished. Repeat around the cake. The top edge of each frill can be decorated with piping or with a crimping tool.

Tip

If you do not have a special frill cutter at home you can easily use individual pastry cutters instead. Use a 3–4 inch plain or fluted cutter to cut out the outer circle and a 1½–2 inch plain cutter to cut out the inner circle.

Design Variations

1 ▲ Looped frills look very pretty attached to the cake "upside-down" as shown here. They are made and attached in the same way as described for looped frills, except that you need to cut out a larger hole from the middle of the ring to make the frills thinner. They will drape more effectively this way.

2 ▲ Frills look equally attractive applied diagonally to the cake sides at regular intervals. They are made and attached to the cake in exactly the same way as described for looped frills, although each ring will probably be large enough to make two frills.

Plaques

A plaque can simply be a plain cut-out shape, or it can be more decorative with, for example, a frilled edge and delicate piping work. Use a plaque as a focal point on a cake to dedicate it to someone special, for a wedding, christening, anniversary or birthday, or as a base on which to paint a picture with food colorings.

1 ▲ To make a plain plaque, roll out the sugarpaste thinly on a work surface lightly dusted with confectioners' sugar. Dip a cutter (round, oval, heart-shaped or fluted) in a little cornstarch. Cut out the shape and leave it to dry flat on waxed paper.

2 ▲ Using royal or glacé icing, pipe on a decoration or name. Alternatively, carefully write or draw on the plaque with a food coloring pen, or with food colorings and a fine paintbrush.

3 ▲ For a frilled plaque, cut out the shape as described above. While the icing is still soft, position the end of a wooden toothpick over about ¼ inch of the outer edge of the plaque. Roll the toothpick back and forth firmly around the edge with your finger. The edge will become thinner and start to frill. Continue until the edge of the plaque is completely frilled.

Endlessly versatile, sugarpaste icing can be embossed, crimped, cut out and marbled, techniques which are all displayed on this unusual diamond-shaped cake. Small cutters have been used for the embossed pattern on the sides, and different crimping tools for the designs at the corners. "Paprika" food coloring has been used for the sugarpaste covering for a contemporary terracotta shade, and the trimmings have been marbled with a little blue icing both for the unusual cut-out edging and the star decorations.

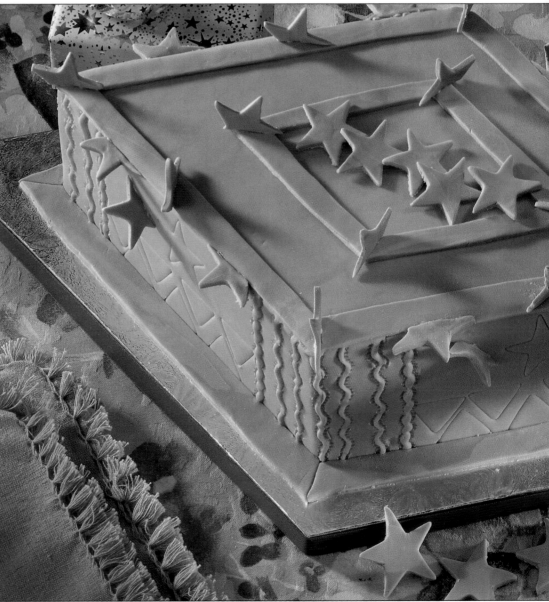

$\mathcal{D}$ecorating with Marzipan

arzipan can be a decorative icing in its own right, or it can provide a firm undercoat for a royal icing or sugarpaste icing covering. It is extremely pliable, and the white variety in particular takes color well.

Marzipan can be molded and shaped, crimped and embossed, and cut out or modeled into all kinds of animal shapes, figures, flowers, fruits, and even edible Christmas decorations, to name just a few possibilities.

Embossing

A "pattern in relief" can be created on cakes by using special embossing tools, or any piece of kitchen equipment that will leave a patterned indentation on the marzipan. To make the embossed picture more interesting, paint on highlights with food coloring.

1 Cover the cake with marzipan, then emboss straight away before the icing dries. Dust the embossing tool with a little cornstarch, press firmly into the marzipan, then lift off carefully to reveal the pattern. Alternatively, for a colored design, brush a little powdered food coloring on to the embossing tool instead of the cornstarch and press on to the marzipan as before.

2 ▼ Paint on colored highlights with food coloring, if you wish.

Very simple versions of crimping and embossing have been applied to the marzipan top of this Simnel cake. The edges are crimped – or fluted – with the fingers and the top is embossed using the back of the fork.

Crimping

As with sugarpaste icing, marzipan can be crimped to give simple, pretty edgings and patterns to cakes.

1 Cover a cake with marzipan, but do not allow it to dry out. To prevent the crimping tool from sticking, dip it in a little cornstarch.

2 Place the crimping tool on the edge of the cake where it is to be decorated and then squeeze the teeth together to make the design. Slowly release the crimping tool, being careful not to let it open quickly or it will tear the marzipan.

3 ▲ Re-position the crimper and repeat to complete the design. You can decorate both the top and base edges of the cake, or the whole side, if you wish. The crimper can also be used to make a pattern on top of the cake.

Marzipan Cut-outs

Small flower and other shaped cutters can be purchased from cake icing specialists for cutting out marzipan shapes. Aspic, cocktail or cookie cutters can also be used. Once you have cut out the basic shapes, you can decorate them with different colored marzipan trims, small sweets or piping. Here are some ideas for cut-out marzipan flowers.

COLORFUL BLOSSOMS

▲ Color the marzipan to the desired shades, then roll it out evenly on a work surface lightly dusted with confectioners' sugar. Dip the ends of a leaf cutter or a small round cutter in cornstarch, and cut out five petals for each flower. Overlap the petals in a circle, securing with a little water. Shape small balls of yellow or orange marzipan and place one in the center of each flower.

FRILLY BLOSSOMS AND LEAVES

▲ Color and roll out the marzipan as for the Colorful Blossoms. For each flower, cut out two circles using two fluted cutters, one slightly smaller than the other. (The sizes will depend on the size of flower you are making.) To frill the edges, position the end of a wooden toothpick over ⅛ inch of the outer edge of each circle. Roll the toothpick firmly back and forth around the edges with your finger so the edges become thinner and begin to frill. Continue until the circles are completely frilled.

Place the smaller frill on top of the larger, and lightly press together to secure. Take a small ball of the deeper shade of marzipan and press through a fine sifter. Cut off the marzipan which has been pushed through the sifter and place in the center of the flower.

Cut out leaves from green marzipan with a leaf cutter. Bend the leaves slightly to make them look more life-like. Larger leaves can be left to bend over the handle of a wooden spoon until firm.

VIOLETS

▲ Color the marzipan purple and roll out as for the Colorful Blossoms. Cut out each flower with a four-petal cocktail cutter. With a little yellow marzipan, shape small balls and then position in the center of each flower.

Creative cut-outs – marzipan can be used in unusual ways to make imaginative shapes and borders.

Modeling

Marzipan is a wonderful icing to use for modeling. Either work with colored marzipan, or use white and highlight it with color after shaping. If coloring your own marzipan, pant it to the required shade, then paint on extra tones and details when the model is assembled to make the objects more life-like. Here are just a few suggestions for shaping fruits and vegetables.

RED-HOT CHILI PEPPERS

▲ Color equal portions of marzipan red and green. Mold the chili shapes, tapering them to a point towards the ends. Shape the stems from green marzipan and attach to the chilies, pressing together lightly to secure.

BUNCH OF GRAPES

▲ Color the marzipan purple. Shape a cone for the main body of the grape bunch, then mold small individual balls for the grapes. Mold the stem, using a little brown marzipan. Arrange the grapes until the cone is completely covered. Use a little water if necessary to make them stick and press lightly to secure. Make a small indentation in the top of the cone and then press in the stem to secure.

RIPE BANANAS

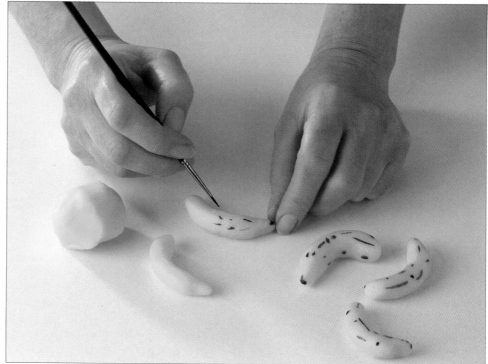

▲ Color the marzipan yellow or use yellow marzipan. Mold and bend small pieces of the icing into the shapes of bananas. Paint on highlights with brown food coloring.

ROSY APPLES

▲ Color the marzipan green for the apples and brown for the stems. Shape the green marzipan into rounds and make an indent at one end with a modeling tool. Shape small pieces of brown icing for the stems. Paint a rosy bloom on the apples with red food coloring and press the stems into the indents.

More familiar as an undercoat for a cake, marzipan should not be neglected as a decoration in itself. It takes color well, and when used to coat this light fruit ring cake, it should certainly not be covered up. Marzipan's plasticity also makes it ideal for molding flowers, such as this colorful collection of roses, and for twisting into ropes to make a colorful edging.

Braiding and Weaving

Use these techniques with marzipan to make colorful edgings and decorations for cakes.

CANDY-STRIPE ROPE

1 Take two pieces of different colored marzipan. On a work surface dusted with confectioners' sugar, roll out two or three ropes of even length and width with your fingers.

2 ▲ Pinch the ends together at the top, then twist into a rope. Pinch the other ends to seal neatly.

BRAID

1 Take three pieces of different colored marzipan. On a work surface dusted with confectioners' sugar, roll out three ropes of even length and width with your fingers.

2 ▲ Pinch the ends together at the top, then braid the ropes neatly and pinch the other ends to seal.

MARZIPAN TWIST

1 Color the marzipan (working with one or two colors). On a work surface dusted with confectioners' sugar, roll out each piece of marzipan to a ¼ inch thickness, then cut each piece into ½ inch wide strips.

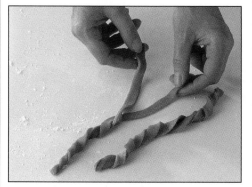

2 ▲ Take two different colored strips and pinch the ends together at the top. Twist the strips together, joining on more strips with water, if needed.

BASKET-WEAVE

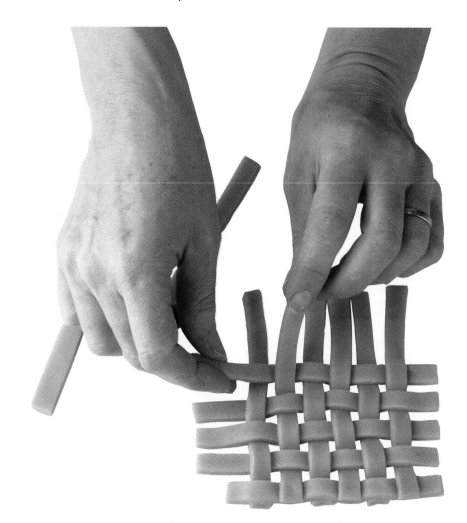

1 ▲ On a work surface lightly dusted with confectioners' sugar, roll out a piece of marzipan (or work with two colors and roll out each one separately) to a ¼ inch thickness. Cut into ¼ inch wide strips.

2 ◄ Arrange the strips, evenly spaced, in parallel lines, then weave the strips in and out. Alternate the colors if using two, as shown. This decoration looks stunning on top of a cake. The edges can be trimmed to fit the shape of the cake.

Marzipan Roses

Not only do these roses smell sweet, they taste good too. Though they may look difficult to make, marzipan roses are quite simple to mold. For a formally decorated cake, shape the roses in a variety of colors and sizes, then arrange flamboyantly on top.

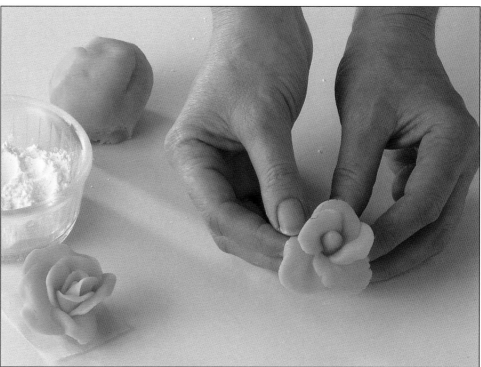

1 ▲ Take a small ball of colored marzipan and form it into a cone shape. This forms the central core which supports the petals.

2 ▲ To make each petal, take a piece of marzipan about the size of a large pea, and work it with your fingers to a petal shape which is slightly thicker at the base. If the marzipan sticks, dust your fingers with cornstarch.

3 ▲ Wrap the petal around the cone as shown. Press the petal to the cone to secure. Bend the ends of the petal back slightly, to curl.

4 ▲ Mold the next petal in the same way and attach as before, so it just overlaps the first one. Curl the ends back slightly. Repeat with several more petals, making them slightly bigger until you have the size of rose you want. Overlap each petal and curl the ends back as before. Make sure all the petals are securely attached, then cut off the base of the cone. This provides a flat surface so the rose will stand on the cake.

5 For rosebuds, make just a few smaller petals and do not curl the ends back.

6 To add more detail to the rose, paint pants on to the petals using a paintbrush and food coloring. Leave to stand on waxed paper until firm.

Blooming roses – molded roses can add glamor to any cake.

ecorating with Butter Icing

Butter icing is very quick to make up and is easy to use for quick and simple decorations. It can be used to sandwich cakes together, or to coat the top and sides with a thick, creamy layer of icing. To make your butter-iced cakes a little more individual, texture the icing on the tops or sides – or both if you wish. To finish, you can pipe the icing in swirls.

Cake Sides

For decorating cake sides, all you need is a plain or serrated scraper, depending on whether you want a smooth or a textured finish to the icing. If you have an icing turntable, it will make icing cake sides a much simpler task, but it is not essential.

Here a chocolate-flavored and green-colored butter icing have been realistically swirled to imitate tree bark and leaves in this delightful novelty cake idea.

1 ▲ Secure the cake to a cake board with a little icing. Cover the top and sides of the cake with icing and put it on an icing turntable. Using a plain or serrated scraper, hold it with one hand firmly against the side of the cake at a slight angle.

2 ▲ Turn the turntable round in a steady continuous motion and in one direction with the other hand, while pulling the scraper smoothly in the opposite direction to give a smooth or serrated surface to the iced sides. When you have completed the full turn, stop the turntable and carefully lift off the scraper to leave a neat join. Trim off any excess icing from the top edge and the cake board.

Cake Tops

More intricate patterns can be made on the tops of cakes with a few simple tools. Use a small spatula, a plain or serrated scraper or a fork to give a silky smooth finish to the cake, or to make a variety of patterned ridges or some deep, generous swirls.

SWIRLS

1 ▲ Spread the icing smoothly over the top of the cake, and then work over the icing with the tip of a spatula from side to side to create a series of swirled grooves.

2 For a more formal appearance, draw the tip of a spatula carefully through the swirled grooves in evenly spaced lines.

RIDGED SPIRAL

1 Spread the icing smoothly over the top of the cake, then place the cake on a turntable.

2 ▲ Hold a serrated scraper at a slight angle, pointing it towards the center of the cake. Rotate the cake with your other hand, while moving the scraper sideways to make undulations and a ridged spiral pattern.

FEATHERED SPIRAL

1 Spread the icing smoothly over the top of the cake and place the cake on a turntable. Rotate the turntable slowly, drawing the flat tip of a spatula in a continuous curved line, starting from the edge of the cake and working in a spiral into the center.

2 ▲ Pull out lines with the tip of the spatula, radiating out from a central point to the edge of the cake.

RIDGED SQUARES

1 Spread the icing smoothly over the top of the cake. Pull a fork across the cake four or five times, depending on the size of the cake, to produce groupings of evenly spaced lines.

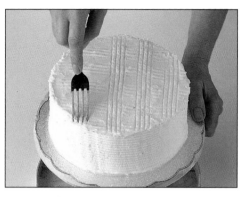

2 ▲ Pull the fork across the cake four or five times as before, but at right angles to the first lines, to give a series of large squares.

DIAMONDS

1 Spread the icing smoothly over the top of the cake. Then lightly dredge with cocoa powder, if using white or lightly tinted butter icing, or confectioners' sugar if using chocolate icing.

2 ▲ Draw a series of lines with the flat side of a spatula to expose the butter icing and to make a diamond pattern over the top.

Piping with Butter Icing

The butter icing needs to be of the correct consistency for piping. To check, dip a spatula and then lift out – the icing should form a sharp point. If too stiff, the icing will be difficult to pipe; if too soft, it will not hold its shape. Add a little extra milk or fruit juice if the consistency is too stiff, or more confectioners' sugar if it is too thin.

DRAMATIC TOUCHES

Piping butter icing in bold, swirling designs with large nozzles can produce dramatic effects.

1 ▲ Cover the top of the cake with a smooth, thin layer of butter icing and smooth the sides with a plain scraper. Using a No 13 plain piping nozzle fitted in a fabric piping bag, pipe large overlapping spirals to cover the top of the cake. For each spiral, start in the center and work outwards, until they are the required size.

2 ▼ Pipe large beads of icing around the edges of the cake, using a large writing nozzle. Lightly sprinkle the spirals with either a little sifted cocoa powder or confectioners' sugar, depending on the color of the butter icing.

DAINTY DESIGNS

For a more delicate effect, use small nozzles to pipe shapes such as dots and beads, stars or scrolls, as demonstrated for royal icing.

1 Cover the top of the cake with a smooth, thin layer of butter icing. Make a ridged pattern with a serrated scraper around the sides of the cake and then a swirled spiral with a spatula over the top.

2 Using a writing nozzle fitted in a paper piping bag, pipe loops and beads of icing in a contrasting color.

3 ▲ Pipe beads of icing at the ends of each loop in the same color as used to cover the cake.

BASKET-WEAVE DESIGN

Butter icing can be piped very effectively with a ribbon nozzle to make a basket-weave design. You can use different colors for the vertical and horizontal lines.

1 Fit a ribbon nozzle into a paper piping bag. Add the icing and fold over the top of the bag to secure. Pipe a vertical line the length of the area you wish to cover with basket weave.

2 Pipe ¾ inch horizontal lines over the vertical line (slightly longer each side than the width of the vertical line) at ½ inch intervals.

3 ▲ Pipe another vertical line so that it just covers one end of all the horizontal lines.

4 ▲ Fill in the spaces between the horizontal lines with an alternating row of horizontal lines to make the basket-weave design. Repeat until the area you wish to cover is completed.

Few can resist the glossy smoothness of butter icing. If you add flavoring and food coloring, the color of the icing should reflect the taste, as with this tangy lemon-iced cake. Use a serrated scraper to create ridges in the icing on the sides and a spatula to make the swirled and feathered effect on the top of the cake. Finish off with generous swirls of piped white butter icing.

ecorating with Glacé Icing

Using white and colored glacé icing, simple but effective patterns can be created for decorating sponges, Madeira cakes or jelly rolls. To vary the ideas shown here using one color of icing, make up two colors of icing and pipe them alternately. Glacé icing sets quickly but needs to be very soft to create the following designs, so make a batch just before you want to decorate the cake and work quickly before it hardens.

Cobweb, Feather and Fan Icing

Cobweb, feather and fan effects are created using the same basic technique. For the cobweb, the colored lines are piped in circles. For the fan, the color is applied in straight lines and the skewer is pulled across in radiating lines. For feather icing the skewer is pulled at right angles through them.

COBWEB ICING

1 Make the glacé icing, color a portion and put in a paper piping bag, as for feather icing. Coat the top of the cake evenly and smoothly with the remaining white icing.

2 ▲ Work quickly before the icing has a chance to set. Pipe evenly spaced circles on top of the icing, starting from the center of the cake and moving towards the edge.

3 ▲ Using a skewer, pull it in straight lines from the edge of the cake to the center so that it is evenly divided into four sections.

4 ▲ Working from the center of the cake to the edge, pull the skewer between the four lines to divide the cake evenly into eight. Leave to set.

For an effective Spider's web cake, use the cobweb icing technique. First cover the cake with yellow glacé icing. Pipe a continuous spiral of black glacé icing, then draw a skewer down from the top at regular intervals.

FEATHER ICING

1 Make the glacé icing (see Basic Icing Recipes). Put 2 tbsp of the icing in a small bowl and color it with a little food coloring.

2 Fit a paper piping bag with a No 2 writing nozzle, then spoon in the colored icing and fold over the top of the bag to secure.

3 ▼ Coat the top of the cake evenly with the remaining white icing. Working quickly so the icing does not set, pipe the colored icing in straight lines across the cake. You may find it easier to work from the center outwards when doing this.

4 ▲ Using a skewer, pull it at right angles through the colored lines in one direction, leaving an even spacing between the lines.

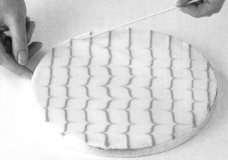

5 ▲ Working in the space between the lines, pull the skewer in the opposite direction, to give a feather pattern. Leave to set.

FAN ICING

1 Make the glacé icing, color a portion and put in a paper piping bag. Ice the top of the cake as for the Feather and Cobweb techniques.

2 Working quickly so the icing does not set, pipe the colored icing in evenly spaced straight lines across the cake. You may find it easier to work from the center outwards.

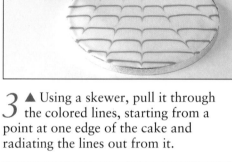

3 ▲ Using a skewer, pull it through the colored lines, starting from a point at one edge of the cake and radiating the lines out from it.

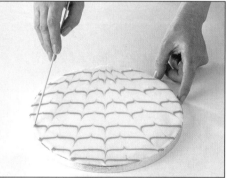

4 ▲ Working in the space between the lines, pull the skewer through the piped lines in the opposite direction to give a fan pattern. Leave to set.

Squiggle Icing

Here a random patterning of icing, similar to cornelli (see Decorating with Royal Icing), is lightly feathered or marbled. The technique is shown here using white icing on a chocolate-tinted background, but would be equally effective using one or two colors on a white icing background.

1 Make the glacé icing. Put 2 tbsp of the icing into a paper piping bag fitted with a No 2 writing nozzle, and color the rest with cocoa mixed with a little water. Coat the top of the cake evenly with the chocolate icing.

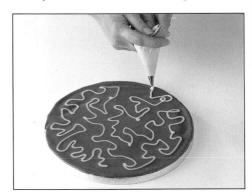

2 ▲ Working quickly before the icing has a chance to set, pipe haphazard squiggles all over the top of the cake in a continuous line.

3 ▼ Using a toothpick, carefully pull it through the lines in short, swirling movements and in different directions, to create a random feathered effect.

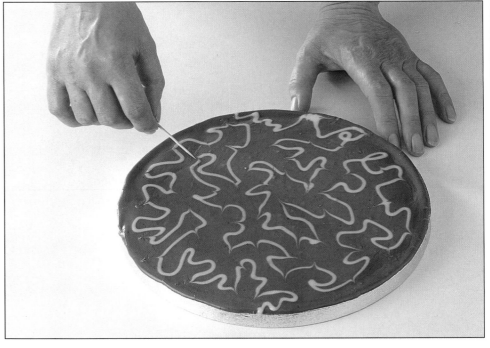

Marbling Flowers and Leaves

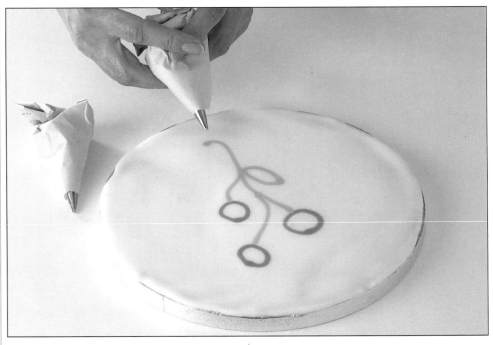

The feathering technique can also be used to give a marbled effect to piped decorations. The technique has been used here for a pretty flower and leaf design. The method is also effective for holly leaves, with the lines being pulled outwards to create the spiky points on the leaves.

1 Make the glacé icing, color a small portion green and a portion red and put each in a paper piping bag fitted with a No 2 writing nozzle. Coat the top of the cake evenly with the remaining white icing.

2 ▲ Working quickly before the icing sets, pipe a floral design on to the cake, piping circles for flowers in the red icing, and ovals for leaves in the green icing.

3 ▲ To marble the flowers, pull a skewer through the lines from the outer edge almost to the middle. The number of petals will be determined by the number of lines you pull. Do the same for the leaves.

Tip

If the top of the cake is not perfectly flat for piping on, simply turn the cake upside down and use the flat base as the top.

Piping with Glacé Icing

All kinds of imaginative designs can be created, using the following method, to decorate the tops and edges of cakes.

This cake is covered with white glacé icing and the side is then coated with green-tinted shredded coconut. The bold, exotic flowers are piped in red and green glacé icing and then marbled with a small toothpick, before the white or colored icings have time to set, for a delicate finish.

1 Make the glacé icing, reserving a few tablespoons for piping. Coat the top of the cake evenly with the remaining icing (either colored or white) and leave to set.

2 Divide the reserved icing into two equal portions and color each in contrasting but complementary shades. Spoon the icings into two separate paper piping bags, each fitted with a No 2 writing nozzle. Use one color to pipe geometric shapes or other simple designs over the icing.

3 ▲ Pipe a border around the edge of the cake with the other color.

Decorating with Chocolate

Nothing adds a luxurious touch to a cake quite like chocolate, whether it is poured over to form a glossy icing, or piped, shaved, dipped or curled. There are several types of chocolate to choose from, and all should be used with care. Couverture is the best and used for professional chocolate work, but it is expensive and requires particularly careful handling. For the following techniques, baking chocolate or eating chocolate are suitable. Chocolate-flavored cake covering is easy to use but is inferior both in taste and texture.

Chocolate decorations can look particularly interesting if different kinds of chocolate – plain, milk and white – are used in combination. White chocolate can be colored, but make sure you use powdered food coloring for this as liquid colorings will thicken it. Store chocolate decorations in the refrigerator in a plastic container between layers of waxed paper until ready to use. Also, handle the decorations as little as possible with your fingers, as they will leave dull marks on the shiny surface of the chocolate and spoil the finished effect.

Melting

For most of the decorations described in this section, the chocolate must be melted first.

1 ▼ Break the chocolate into small pieces and place in a bowl set over a pan of hot water. Do not allow the bowl to touch the water and do not let the water boil; the chocolate will spoil if overheated. Melt the chocolate slowly and stir occasionally. Be careful not to let water or steam near the chocolate or it will become too thick.

2 ▲ When the chocolate is completely melted, remove the pan from the heat and stir.

Coating Cakes

1 ▲ Stand the cake on a wire rack. It is a good idea to place a sheet of waxed paper or a baking sheet underneath the rack to catch any chocolate drips. Pour the chocolate over the cake quickly, in one smooth motion, to coat the top and sides.

2 Use a spatula to smooth the chocolate over the sides, if necessary. Allow the chocolate to set, then coat with another layer, if wished.

Piping with Chocolate

Chocolate can be piped directly on to a cake, or it can be piped on to parchment paper to make run-outs, small outlined shapes or irregular designs. After melting the chocolate, allow it to cool slightly so it just coats the back of a spoon. If it still flows freely it will be too runny to hold its shape when piped. When it is the right consistency, you then need to work fast as the chocolate will set quickly.

CHOCOLATE OUTLINES

Pipe the chocolate in small, delicate shapes to use as elegant decorations on cakes. Or pipe random squiggles and loosely drizzle a contrasting chocolate over the top.

1 Melt 4 oz chocolate and allow to cool slightly. Tape a piece of parchment paper to a baking sheet or flat board.

2 ▼ Fill a paper piping bag with the chocolate. Cut a small piece off the pointed end of the bag in a straight line. Pipe your chosen shape in a continuous line, and repeat or vary. Leave to set in a cool place, then carefully lift off the paper with a spatula.

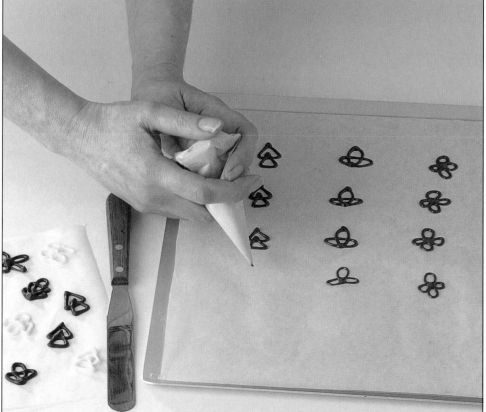

PIPING ON TO CAKES

This looks effective on top of a cake iced with coffee glacé icing.

1 Melt 2 oz each of white and plain chocolate in separate bowls and allow to cool slightly. Place the chocolates in separate paper piping bags. Cut a small piece off the pointed end of each bag in a straight line.

2 ▲ Hold each piping bag in turn above the surface of the cake and pipe the chocolates all over. Here, the chocolates have been piped in overlapping semi-circles of different sizes. Try your own designs, too.

CHOCOLATE LACE CURLS

Make lots of these curly shapes and store them in a cool place ready for using as cake decorations. Try piping the lines in contrasting colors of chocolate to vary the effect.

1 ▲ Melt 4 oz chocolate and allow to cool slightly. Cover a rolling pin with parchment paper and attach it with tape. Fill a paper piping bag with the chocolate and cut a small piece off the pointed end in a straight line.

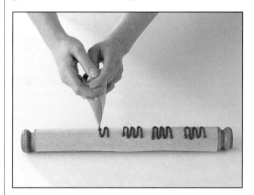

2 ▲ Pipe lines of chocolate backwards and forwards over the parchment paper, as shown.

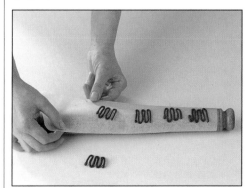

3 ▲ Leave the chocolate lace curls to set in a cool place, then carefully peel off the paper.

Marbling Chocolate _ Chocolate Run-outs

Here, plain chocolate is swirled over a white glacé-iced cake for a stunningly simple effect. Before melting the chocolate, make the icing, then work very quickly while both the chocolate and the icing are still soft.

1 Melt 2 oz plain chocolate. Coat the top of the cake evenly and smoothly with white glacé icing.

2 ▲ Spoon the chocolate into a paper piping bag, cut a small piece off the pointed end in a straight line and then quickly pipe the chocolate in large, loose loops.

3 ▼ Pull a toothpick through the chocolate in short, swirling movements and in different directions, to create a random marbled effect.

The same basic method used for making royal icing run-outs is used here with chocolate. Try piping the outline in one color of chocolate and then filling in the middle with another.

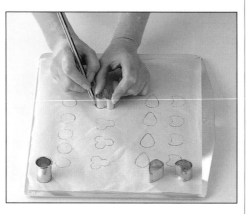

1 ▲ Tape a piece of waxed paper to a baking sheet or flat board. Draw around a shaped cookie cutter on to the paper, or trace or draw a shape of your choice freehand. Repeat the design several times.

2 Secure a piece of parchment paper over the top of the penciled design. Tape it down securely at the corners with masking tape.

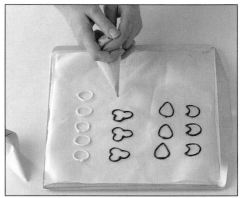

3 ▲ Fill two paper piping bags with melted chocolate. Cut a small piece off the pointed end of one of the bags in a straight line and pipe over the outline of your design in a continuous thread.

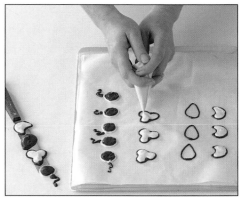

4 ▲ Cut the end off the other bag, slightly wider than before, and pipe the chocolate to fill in the outline so it looks slightly rounded. Leave to set in a cool place, then carefully lift off the paper with a spatula.

Chocolate icing and decorating techniques are demonstrated in all their glory on this sumptuous chocolate gâteau. The cake is covered with fudge frosting. A neat ring of cocoa is then dusted around the edge, using a round stencil to protect the center of the cake. The cake is decorated with mottled white and plain chocolate leaves. Chocolate curls adorn the top, and haphazardly piped white chocolate shapes, loosely overpiped with plain chocolate, complete the ultimate chocoholic extravaganza.

Chocolate Leaves

Chocolate leaves are made by coating real leaves with plain, white or milk chocolate or any combination of the three. Choose small freshly-picked leaves with simple shapes and well-defined veins, such as rose leaves. Leave a short stem on the leaves so you have something to hold.

1 ▲ Wash and dry the leaves well on paper towels. Melt 4 oz chocolate. Using a paintbrush, brush the underside of each leaf with chocolate. Take care not to go over the edge of the leaf or the chocolate will be difficult to peel off.

2 ▲ Using different chocolates for a mottled effect, brush the leaves in the same way, partly with plain or milk and partly with white chocolate.

3 Place the leaves chocolate-side up on parchment paper. Leave to set.

4 ▲ Carefully peel the leaf from the chocolate, handling the chocolate as little as possible. If the chocolate seems too thin, re-coat with more melted chocolate. Leave to set.

Chocolate Cut-outs

You can make abstract shapes, or circles, squares and diamonds, by cutting them out freehand with a sharp knife. Alternatively, use a large cookie cutter or ruler as a guide, or cut out the shapes with small cookie or cocktail cutters. These shapes look equally attractive whether evenly positioned around the sides of the cake, spaced apart or overlapping each other, or simply arranged haphazardly.

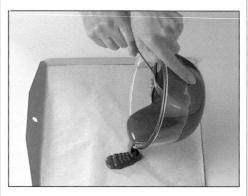

1 ▲ Cover a baking sheet with parchment paper and tape down at each corner. Melt 4 oz plain, milk or white chocolate. Pour the chocolate on to the parchment paper.

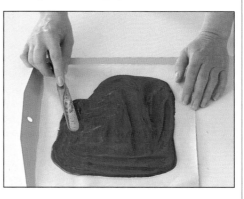

2 ▲ Spread the chocolate evenly with a spatula. Allow to stand until the surface is firm enough to cut, but not so hard that it will break. It should no longer feel sticky when touched with your finger.

3 ▲ Press the cutter firmly through the chocolate and lift off the paper with a spatula. Try not to touch the surface of the chocolate or you will leave marks on it.

4 ▲ The finished shapes can be left plain or piped with a contrasting chocolate if you wish.

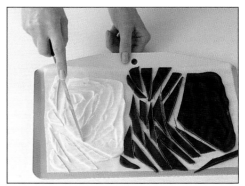

5 ▲ Abstract shapes can be cut with a sharp knife freehand. They look particularly effective pressed on to the sides of a butter iced cake.

Chocolate-dipped Fruit and Nuts

Use small, fresh fruit such as strawberries, grapes and kumquats for dipping, and whole nuts such as almonds, cashews, brazils or macadamias. Make sure that the fruit and nuts are at room temperature, or the chocolate will set too quickly.

1 Line a baking sheet with parchment paper. Wash the fruit and dry well on paper towels. Hold the fruit by its stem, then dip into the chocolate. You can either coat the piece of fruit completely, or just dip half of it, leaving the line of chocolate straight or at a slight angle. Remove the fruit, shake it gently and let any excess chocolate fall back into the bowl. Place on parchment paper and leave to set.

2 ▲ For nuts, place a nut on the end of a long kitchen fork or dipping fork. Lower into the chocolate and coat completely. Lift out of the chocolate and shake off any excess, then leave to set as for fruit. To coat just half of the nut, hold it between your fingers and dip part way into the chocolate.

3 For a two-tone effect, melt plain and white chocolate in separate bowls. Dip the fruit or nuts into one color to coat completely, then, when set, half-dip into the other color.

Chocolate Curls

1 Melt 4 oz chocolate. Pour the chocolate on to a firm, smooth surface such as a marble, wood or formica, set on a slightly damp cloth to prevent slipping. Spread the chocolate evenly and smoothly over the surface with a large spatula.

2 ▲ Leave the chocolate to cool slightly. It should feel just set, but not hard. Hold a large sharp knife at a 45° angle to the chocolate and push it along the chocolate in short sawing movements from right to left and left to right to make curls.

3 ▲ Remove the curls by sliding the point of the knife underneath each one and lifting off. Leave until firm.

Chocolate Shavings

The quickest way to turn chocolate into a decoration is simply to grate or shave it. The chocolate should be at room temperature for this.

1 ▲ For fine shavings, grate the chocolate on the coarse side of a grater. For coarser shavings, peel off curls with a vegetable peeler.

This sophisticated heart-shaped cake is a wonderful idea for Valentine's Day or to celebrate an engagement. It is completely covered with rich, plain chocolate curls.

COLOR EFFECTS

*If you think of the surface of a cake as an artist's canvas, it opens up
all sorts of decorating ideas using painting and drawing techniques.
This is made possible by the wide range of colors available in the form
of food colorings and food coloring pens.*

Using Stencils

Cards with stencil patterns on them can be found at cake icing specialists or at stationers, or you can make your own stencils out of thin cardboard.

1 Coat the cake with sugarpaste, royal or marzipan icing and leave to dry.

2 ▲ Lay the stencil over the surface of the cake. Dip a completely dry, clean paintbrush into some powdered food coloring and dab into the stencil. Lift off the stencil to reveal the design. You could also fill in the color with a food coloring pen.

Flicking

Use one color or several. This is almost a decoration in itself.

1 Cover the cake with sugarpaste, royal or marzipan icing and leave to dry. Place the cake on a fairly large sheet of waxed paper to protect the work surface.

2 ▲ Water down the food coloring, and then load up the end of the paintbrush with the color. Position the brush over the area you wish to color, then flick your wrist in the direction of the cake, so the color falls on to it in small beads.

Linework

Food coloring pens are a quick way to add simple line designs to the tops and sides of cakes. Use a ruler to achieve straight lines, and a pair of compasses for large curved lines.

1 Cover the cake and leave to dry. Royal icing gives the firmest surface for the pens. Work out the design.

2 ▲ For small circles, curves or semi-circles, draw around the edge of a plain round cutter.

3 ▼ Add details to the design with small dots.

Painting and Drawing

Food colorings can be used like water-colors and food coloring pens like crayons or felt-tip pens on iced cakes. Let the icing dry before applying the design. Before working on the cake, you might find it easier to practice on a spare piece of icing. When painting different colors next to each other, allow the first color to dry before applying the second to prevent colors running into each other – unless that is the effect you wish to achieve.

1 ▲ Dilute food colorings with a little water or use straight from the bottle. A small plastic palette is useful for mixing the colors. Work out the design and either paint it straight on to the cake, or draw it out first with a food coloring pen.

2 ▲ Food coloring pens look like felt-tip pens, but are filled with edible food colorings. They are a speedy way to add lively highlights to designs. They can also be used to color in patterned borders, to draw personalized pictures or to write messages.

3 ►Look to the great artists, such as Matisse and Picasso, for inspiration, either for a painting style or theme.

Stippling

This is normally used as a background decoration, so it is best to keep the colors delicate. Try blending two soft shades together.

1 Cover the cake with sugarpaste, royal or marzipan icing and leave until the icing is dry.

2 ▲ Water down the food coloring and apply with a dry, clean piece of sponge or paper towel, by dabbing it on to the surface of the cake.

Powdered Tints

These can be brushed on dry, either with a paintbrush for detail, or with a clean, dry piece of sponge when you wish to cover larger areas.

1 Cover the cake with sugarpaste, royal or marzipan icing and leave until the icing is dry.

2 ▲ Draw on the design with different colored food coloring pens, and then brush in the colors with powdered tints.

Using Bought Decorations

When you want to put a cake together in a hurry for a last-minute celebration, or even if you do not have much time to spend on decorating cakes, remember there are all kinds of easy-to-use edible items and ready-to-use decorations that can be found in supermarkets, health food shops, and in confectionery and specialist cake icing shops.

Edible Decorations

Here are just some of the delicious edible decorations which can be used for quick-and-easy cake decorating. Keep a few of these in your cupboard, ready for an impromptu celebration cake.

Candies Choose small, colorful, simple shapes such as jelly babies, jellybeans, colored chocolate beans, chocolate buttons, liquorice gum drops, chocolate-coated espresso beans, yogurt-coated nuts and raisins, small molded chocolate shapes or sugared almonds. These are just a few of the candies which, used with imagination and flair, turn a cake into something special.
Jellied Shapes Packaged jellied orange and lemon slices are also useful, either whole or cut into wedges, as are jelly diamonds, available in several colors.
Nuts Use these chopped or whole, plain or toasted, for decorating the tops and to coat the sides of cakes.
Glacé and Crystallized Fruits Glacé cherries and angelica are probably the most familiar of these popular quick cake decorations, but there are many other tasty varieties to choose from, such as pineapple and ginger – even diced papaya. Depending on their size, the fruits can be halved, sliced, chopped or cut into shapes ready for arranging on the cake.
Coconut Shredded coconut is another useful cake decoration, particularly as it can also be panted with a few drops of food coloring to give an attractive coating for the sides of a cake. Other more unusual kinds of coconut are also available, such as coconut threads, coconut chips and coconut slices. All can be used raw or toasted.

Marzipan Fruits and Sugar Flowers Both can be bought ready-made if you do not wish to shape your own.
Citrus Fruits Fresh lemon, lime and orange zest can be transformed into attractive cake decorations. Cut off thin, curly strips of rind with a sharp knife or zester. Alternatively, use pany aspic cutters to cut out shapes from the rinds, but be careful not to include the white pith. The shapes can be grouped together or linked to form a border around the cake.

MAKING PATTERNS WITH EDIBLE DECORATIONS

1 ▲ Arrange jelly diamonds and jellied orange slices on a square or round cake to form a pretty stylized design such as the one shown.

2 ▲ This jazzy design is ideal for a child's cake. It is made from whole and halved colored chocolate beans.

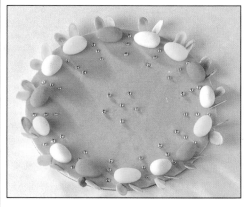

3 ▲ Sugared almonds, flaked toasted almonds and silver balls add life to any cake iced in pastel shades, and are ideal for Easter.

Decorative edibles help to make cake decorating fun as well as easy.

Candy Flowers

Edible decorations can be used in different combinations to make attractive floral designs for cakes.

1 ▲ Use jelly diamonds for the petals and leaves, slices of colored candies for the centers and strips of angelica for the stems.

2 ▲ Arrange halved colored chocolate beans, cut-side down, to form a flower. Use different colors, with a silver ball for the center.

3 ▲ Dip blanched whole almonds in melted chocolate to form the petals of a flower, then arrange with a chocolate button or chocolate bean for the center.

Stenciling

For this technique you can use confectioners' sugar, cocoa or finely ground nuts to create the stenciling effect.

1 ▲ For a quick stenciled pattern, lay a patterned doiley on the cake and sift confectioners' sugar over it, then lift off the doiley. The center can be cut out of the doiley to create another stenciled area. For maximum color contrast, use confectioners' sugar on a chocolate cake and cocoa on a plain cake.

2 ▼ Another stenciling method is to lay strips of paper over the cake, either in straight lines, diagonally or in a lattice pattern. Use fairly thick paper so it lies flat. For more dramatic effects, cut out strips of paper in wavy, zigzag or other geometric patterns.

It's time to have fun. Load up a paintbrush with orange food coloring and then flick it over a sugarpaste-iced cake. Cut out bears with the icing and paint on their features. Line up jelly teddy bears, jellybeans and other colorful candies, paint a bright design on the iced board and you have a cake that is surprisingly easy to decorate.

Ribbon Decorations

Stripy ones, dotty ones, sparkly ones, wide and pencil-thin ones – ribbons are a lovely way to add height, color and a special celebratory look to a cake. They can be wrapped around the cake, using varying widths and colors for different effects, made into simple shapes, or threaded into the icing. Tiny colored bows can be purchased from cake icing specialists, or you can make your own decorations as suggested here.

RIBBON LOOPS

These look pretty if one or several loops are attached to florists' wire, or if alternating colors are looped together.

1 Use a length of thin ribbon, about ¼ inch wide. Make two or three small loops of ribbon.

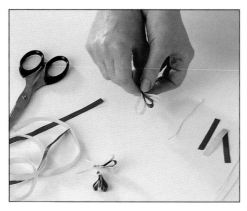

2 ▲ Using a piece of florists' wire, twist it around the ends of the ribbon to secure the loops together. Trim the ends of the ribbon. The wire will form a stem for the loops, so cut it to the required length and use it to put the loops in position on the cake. The loops must be removed from the cake before serving.

RIBBON CURLS

▲ Use a thin piece of gift wrapping ribbon, about ¼ inch wide, and cut into the chosen lengths. Run the blade of a pair of scissors or a sharp knife down the length of the ribbons to make them curl.

MULTIPLE CURLS

▲ Use a thick piece of gift wrapping ribbon, about ¾ inch wide, and cut into the chosen lengths. Tear the ribbon into four or five thin strips, almost to the end. Run the blade of a pair of scissors or a sharp knife down the length of each strip to curl.

OVALS

▲ Hold both ends of a thin piece of ribbon. With your left hand bring the end up and twist it over to cross and form an oval with two straight ends hanging down. Where the ribbon crosses, secure with a little royal icing. Cut the ends diagonally to neaten.

RIBBON DESIGNS

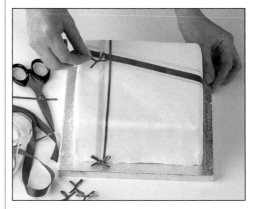

▲ Use combinations of colors and widths of ribbons and bows to create special patterns on the tops and sides of cakes. Secure with a little royal icing.

A riot of ribbons – let the colors or patterns of ribbon you choose complement the shade and design of the cake without dominating it.

RIBBON INSERTION

This technique looks much more difficult than it actually is. A cake covered with sugarpaste icing provides the best surface for this decoration. Leave the icing to dry until it is soft underneath and just firm on the top.

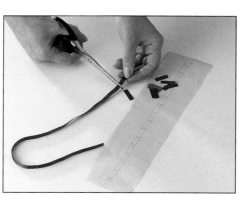

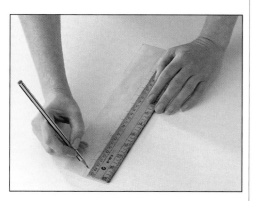

1 ▲ Work out your design for the number and size of slits, and whether the design is to be straight or curved. Draw the design on a piece of waxed paper.

2 ▲ Cut pieces of ribbon which are fractionally longer than the size of each slit.

3 ▲ Secure the template to the cake with pins. Cut through the drawn lines to make the slits in the icing using a scalpel. Remove the template.

4 ▲ With the aid of a pointed tool, insert one end of the ribbon into the first slit and the other end into the second slit.

5 ▲ Leave a space and repeat, filling all the slits with the pieces of ribbon in the same way.

Sugar-frosting Flowers and Fruit

Something as simple as a spray of fresh sugar-frosted flowers or a grouping of small fruits is often all that is needed to decorate a cake. When frosting flowers choose ones that are edible, such as pansies, primroses, violets, roses, freesias, pany daffodils or nasturtiums.

FLOWERS

Sugar-frosted flowers keep surprisingly well, and you may want to make the most of springtime primroses and violets to liven up cakes later in the year. Once the flowers are dry, store them in a single layer between sheets of tissue paper in a small box. Keep the box in a cool, dry place.

Frosty florals – whole flowers or individual petals can be frosted in the same way.

1 ▲ Lightly whisk an egg white in a small bowl, and sprinkle some superfine sugar on to a plate. Dry the flower on paper towels. If possible, leave some stem attached. Evenly brush both sides of the petals with egg white.

2 ▲ Holding the flower by its stem over a plate lined with paper towels, sprinkle it evenly with the sugar, then shake off any excess.

3 ▲ Place on a flat board or wire rack covered with paper towels and leave to dry in a warm place.

FRUITS

When frosting fruits, choose really fresh ones which are small and firm such as kumquats, cherries, grapes or strawberries. Frosted fruits will only keep as long as the fruits themselves stay fresh. Place on a lined tray and keep in the refrigerator. Eat within two days.

1 Wash the fruit and then pat dry on paper towels.

2 ▲ Lightly whisk an egg white in a small bowl, and sprinkle some superfine sugar on to a plate. Hold the fruit by the stem if possible and evenly brush all over with the egg white.

Sometimes the simplest cakes can be the most elegant. The stark white background of sugarpaste icing is all that is needed to show off a sweeping spray of frosted flowers, an interlocking design of ribbons and a few ribbon curls and bows.

3 ▲ Holding the fruit over a plate lined with paper towels, sprinkle it evenly with the sugar, then shake off any excess.

4 Place on a flat board or wire rack covered with paper towels and leave to dry in a warm place.

Frosty fruits – make a pile of these luscious fruits for a stunning centerpiece on a cake.

Classic Cakes

Classic Cakes includes innovative interpretations and designs for much-loved favorites which are a must for every cake-maker's basic repertoire. From simply decorated sponge cakes, to delicious dessert cakes and sumptuous gâteaux, there are recipes here for every taste and every occasion.

One-stage Victoria Sandwich

Originally made in an oblong shape, today's Victoria sandwich is made using a variety of different flavorings and decorations, and is baked and cut into all sorts of shapes and sizes. Use this basic recipe to suit the occasion.

INGREDIENTS
Serves 6–8
1½ cups self-rising flour
pinch of salt
¾ cup butter, softened
¾ cup superfine sugar
3 large eggs

To Finish
4–6 tbsp raspberry jam
superfine or confectioners' sugar

STORING
This cake can be stored for up to three days in an airtight container.

1 Preheat the oven to 375°F. Grease two deep 7 inch round cake pans, line the bases with waxed paper and grease the paper.

2 ▲ Place all the ingredients in a mixing bowl and whisk together using electric beaters. Divide the mixture between the prepared pans and smooth the surfaces. Bake in the center of the oven for 25–30 minutes, or until a skewer inserted into the center of the cakes comes out clean. Turn out on to a wire rack, peel off the lining paper and leave to cool completely.

3 ▲ Place one of the cakes on a serving plate and spread with the raspberry jam. Place the other cake on top, then dredge with superfine or confectioners' sugar, to serve.

Variation
Makes 8–10 iced fancies

1 ▲ Place the cake mixture in a greased and lined 9 x 13 inch jelly roll pan and smooth the surface. Bake in the center of the oven for 25–30 minutes, or until a skewer inserted into the center of the cake comes out clean. Turn out on to a wire rack, peel off the lining paper and leave to cool completely.

2 ▲ Cut the cake into individual sized shapes, such as fingers, diamonds, squares or small rounds, using a knife or cookie cutters. Using one quantity of Butter Icing, cover with decorative piping. You can flavor or color the butter icing by substituting orange or lemon juice for the milk and/or adding a few drops of food coloring.

3 For alternative decorations, you could try a selection of the following: glacé cherries, angelica, jellied fruits, grated chocolate, chopped or whole nuts, or choose one of your own ideas.

Tip

To make the decorative stenciled pattern with confectioners' sugar shown here, cut out star shapes from paper. Lay the paper stars over the top of the cake and then dredge with confectioners' sugar. Remove the paper shapes carefully to reveal the stenciled pattern. You could also use a paper doily as a stencil.

Flourless Fruit Cake

A really easy recipe which everyone will enjoy. Children can have fun crushing the cornflakes and helping you to beat the ingredients together.

INGREDIENTS
Serves 12–15
1 x 1 lb jar mincemeat
2 cups dried mixed fruit
1 cup no-soak,
ready-to-eat dried apricots, chopped
1 cup no-soak, ready-to-eat dried
figs, chopped
½ cup glacé cherries, halved
1 cup walnut pieces
8–10 cups cornflakes, crushed
4 large eggs, lightly beaten
1 x 14½ oz can evaporated milk
1 tsp ground allspice
1 tsp baking powder
mixed glacé fruits, chopped,
to decorate

STORING
This cake can be kept for up to a week in an airtight container.

1 Preheat the oven to 300°F. Grease a 10 inch round cake pan, line the base and sides with a double thickness of waxed paper and grease the paper.

2 Put all the ingredients into a large mixing bowl. Beat together well.

3 ▲ Turn into the prepared pan and smooth the surface with the back of a spoon.

4 ▲ Bake in the center of the oven for about 1¾ hours, or until a skewer inserted in the center of the cake comes out clean. Allow the cake to cool in the pan for 10 minutes, then turn out on to a wire rack, peel off the lining paper and leave to cool completely. Decorate with the chopped glacé fruits.

Tip

This cake may be iced and marzipanned to make a Christmas or birthday cake. A useful recipe for anyone who needs to avoid eating wheat flour.

ooseberry Cake

*This cake is delicious served warm
with fresh whipped cream.*

INGREDIENTS
Serves 6–8
½ cup butter
1⅓ cups self-rising flour
1 tsp baking powder
2 large eggs, beaten
½ cup superfine sugar
1–2 tsp rose water
pinch of freshly grated nutmeg
1 x 4 oz jar gooseberries in syrup,
drained, juice reserved
superfine sugar, to decorate
whipped cream, to serve

STORING
*This cake can be kept for up to
three days in an airtight container.*

1 Preheat the oven to 350°F. Grease a 7 inch square cake pan, line the base and sides with waxed paper and then grease the paper.

2 Place the butter in a medium saucepan and melt over a gentle heat. Remove the pan from the heat, transfer the melted butter to a mixing bowl and allow to cool.

3 ▲ Sift together the flour and baking powder and add to the melted butter. Beat in the eggs, one at a time, the sugar, rose water and grated nutmeg, to make a smooth batter.

4 ▲ Mix in 1–2 tbsp of the reserved gooseberry juice, then pour half of the batter mixture into the prepared pan. Scatter over the gooseberries. Pour over the remaining batter mixture, evenly covering the gooseberries.

5 Bake in the center of the oven for about 45 minutes, or until a skewer inserted into the center of the cake comes out clean.

6 ▲ Leave in the cake pan for about 5 minutes, then turn out on to a wire rack, remove the lining paper and allow to cool for a further 5 minutes. Dredge with superfine sugar and serve immediately with whipped cream, or leave the cake to cool completely before decorating and serving.

Lemon and Apricot Cake

This tasty cake is topped with a crunchy layer of flaked almonds and pistachio nuts, and is soaked in a tangy lemon syrup after baking to keep it really moist.

INGREDIENTS
Serves 10–12
¾ *cup butter, softened*
1½ *cups self-rising flour, sifted*
½ *tsp baking powder*
¾ *cup superfine sugar*
3 *large eggs, lightly beaten*
finely grated zest of 1 lemon
1½ *cups no-soak, ready-to-eat dried apricots, finely chopped*
1 *cup ground almonds*
⅓ *cup unsalted pistachio nuts, chopped*
⅓ *cup flaked almonds*
2 *tbsp unsalted whole pistachio nuts*

For the Syrup
freshly squeezed juice of 1 lemon
3 *tbsp superfine sugar*

STORING
This cake can be kept for up to three days in an airtight container.

1 Preheat the oven to 350°F. Grease a 2 lb loaf pan, line the base and sides with waxed paper and grease the paper.

2 Place the butter together with the sifted flour and baking powder into a mixing bowl, then add the sugar, eggs and lemon zest. Beat for 1–2 minutes until smooth and glossy, and then stir in the apricots, ground almonds and the chopped pistachio nuts.

3 ▲ Spoon the mixture into the prepared pan and smooth the surface. Sprinkle with the flaked almonds and the whole pistachio nuts. Bake in the center of the oven for about 1¼ hours, or until a skewer inserted into the center of the cake comes out clean. Check the cake after about 45 minutes and cover with a piece of foil when the top is nicely brown. Leave the cake to cool in the pan.

4 ▲ To make the lemon syrup, put the lemon juice and superfine sugar into a small saucepan and heat gently, stirring until the sugar has dissolved.

5 ▲ Spoon the syrup over the cake. When the cake is completely cooled, turn it carefully out of the pan and peel off the lining paper.

Cherry Batter Cake

This colorful tray bake looks pretty cut into neat squares or fingers.

INGREDIENTS
Serves 8–10
2 cups self-rising flour
1 tsp baking powder
6 tbsp butter, softened
²⁄₃ cup soft light brown sugar, firmly
packed
1 large egg, lightly beaten
²⁄₃ cup milk

For the Topping
1 x 1½ lb jar black cherries or black
currants, drained
¾ cup soft light brown sugar, firmly
packed
½ cup self-rising flour
4 tbsp butter, melted
sifted confectioners' sugar,
to decorate
whipped cream, to serve (optional)

STORING
*This cake can be kept for up to two
days in an airtight container.*

1 Preheat the oven to 375°F. Grease a
13 x 9 inch jelly roll pan, line the
base and sides with waxed paper and
grease the paper.

2 To make the base, sift the flour and
baking powder into a mixing bowl.
Add the butter, sugar, egg and milk.
Beat the mixture until the batter
becomes smooth, then turn into the
prepared pan and smooth the surface.

3 ▲ Scatter the drained fruit evenly
over the batter mixture.

4 ▲ Mix together the remaining
topping ingredients and spoon
evenly over the fruit. Bake in the center
of the oven for about 40 minutes, or
until golden brown and the center is
firm to the touch.

5 Leave to cool, then dredge with
confectioners' sugar. Serve with
whipped cream, if wished.

Carrot and Almond Cake

*Made with grated carrots and ground almonds, this unusual
fat-free sponge cake makes a delicious afternoon treat.*

INGREDIENTS
Serves 8–10
5 large eggs, separated
finely grated zest of 1 lemon
1⅓ cups superfine sugar
5–6 medium-size carrots, peeled and
finely grated
1¼ cups ground almonds
1 cup self-rising flour, sifted
sifted confectioners' sugar, to
decorate
marzipan carrots, to decorate

STORING
*This cake can be kept for up to two
days in an airtight container.*

Tip

To make the marzipan carrots,
knead a little orange food coloring
into 4 oz marzipan until evenly
blended. On a work surface lightly
dusted with confectioners' sugar,
divide the marzipan into even-sized
pieces, about the size of small walnuts. Mold into carrot shapes and
press horizontal lines along each
carrot with a knife blade. Press a
tiny stick of angelica into the end of
each piece to resemble the carrot
top. Position the marzipan carrots
on the cake, to decorate.

1 Preheat the oven to 375°F. Grease
a deep 8 inch round cake pan, line
the base with waxed paper and grease
the paper.

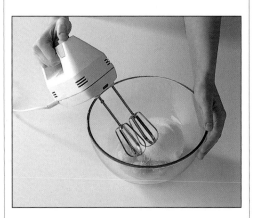

2 ▲ Place the egg yolks, lemon zest
and sugar in a bowl. Beat with
electric beaters for about 5 minutes,
until the mixture is thick and pale.

3 ▲ Mix in the grated carrot, ground
almonds and flour and stir until
evenly combined.

4 In a clean, dry bowl, whisk the egg
whites until stiff. Using a large
metal spoon or rubber spatula, mix a
little of the whisked egg whites into the
carrot mixture, then fold in the rest.

5 ▲ Spoon the mixture into the
prepared cake pan and bake in the
center of the oven for about 1¼ hours,
or until a skewer inserted into the
center of the cake comes out clean.
Leave the cake in the pan for about
5 minutes, then turn out on to a wire
rack, peel off the lining paper and leave
to cool completely.

6 ▲ Decorate with sifted confectioners' sugar and marzipan carrots.

Banana Coconut Cake

*Slightly over-ripe bananas are best for
this perfect coffee morning cake.*

INGREDIENTS
Serves 8–10
1½ cups shredded coconut
½ cup butter, softened
½ cup superfine sugar
2 large eggs
1 cup self-rising flour
½ cup flour
1 tsp baking soda
½ cup milk
2 large bananas, peeled and mashed

For the Topping
2 tbsp butter
2 tbsp honey
2 cups shredded coconut

STORING
*This cake will keep for up to two
days in an airtight container.*

1 Preheat the oven to 375°F. Grease a
deep 7 inch square cake pan, line
the base and sides with waxed paper
and then grease the paper.

2 ▲ Spread the shredded coconut out
on a baking sheet and place under a
hot broiler for about 5 minutes, stirring
and turning the coconut all the time
until evenly toasted.

3 Place the butter and sugar in a
mixing bowl and beat until they are
smooth and creamy. Beat in the eggs,
one at a time.

4 Sift together the flours and baking
soda, then sift half of this mixture
into the butter and egg mixture and stir
to mix thoroughly.

5 Mix together the milk and mashed
banana in a small bowl, then add
half to the egg mixture. Beat well to
combine, then add the remaining flour
and toasted coconut together with the
remaining banana mixture. Stir to mix,
then transfer to the prepared cake pan
and smooth the surface.

6 Bake in the center of the oven for
about 1 hour, or until a skewer
inserted into the center of the cake
comes out clean. Leave the cake in the
pan for about 5 minutes, then turn out
on to a wire rack, peel off the lining
paper and leave to cool completely.

7 To make the topping, place the
butter and honey in a small
saucepan and heat gently until melted.
Stir in the shredded coconut and cook,
stirring constantly, for about 5 minutes
or until lightly browned. Remove from
the heat and allow to cool slightly.

8 ▲ Spoon the topping over the top
of the cake and allow to cool
completely before serving.

Almond and Apricot Cake

Although canned apricots can be used in this recipe, nothing quite beats using the fresh fruit in season. Choose sweet-smelling, ripe fruit for this delicious cake.

INGREDIENTS
Serves 6–8
4–5 tbsp fine dry white bread crumbs
1 cup butter, softened
1 cup plus 2 tbsp superfine sugar
4 large eggs
1½ cups self-rising flour
1–2 tbsp milk
1⅓ cups ground almonds
few drops of almond extract
1 lb fresh apricots, pitted and halved
sifted superfine sugar, to decorate

STORING
This cake can be kept for up to three days in an airtight container.

3 ▲ Place the butter and sugar in a mixing bowl and beat with electric beaters until light and fluffy. Beat in the eggs, one at a time, then fold in the flour, milk, ground almonds and almond extract.

4 ▲ Spoon half of the cake mixture into the prepared pan and smooth the surface. Arrange half of the apricots over the top, then spoon over the remaining cake mixture. Finish with the other half of the apricots. Bake the cake in the center of the oven for 30–35 minutes, or until a skewer inserted into the center of the cake comes out clean.

5 Turn the cake out on to a wire rack, peel off the lining paper and sprinkle over the sifted superfine sugar. Serve warm or leave to cool.

1 Preheat the oven to 350°F. Grease a 9 inch round cake pan, line the base with waxed paper and grease the paper.

2 ▲ Sprinkle the bread crumbs into the prepared cake pan and tap them around the pan to coat the base and sides evenly.

Jewel Cake

This pretty tea-time cake is excellent
served as an afternoon snack with tea or coffee.

INGREDIENTS
Serves 10–15
½ cup mixed colored glacé cherries,
halved, washed and dried
¼ cup preserved ginger in syrup,
chopped, washed and dried
⅓ cup chopped mixed citrus peel
1 cup self-rising flour
¾ cup flour
3 tbsp cornstarch
¾ cup butter
¾ cup superfine sugar
3 large eggs
finely grated zest of 1 orange

To Decorate
1½ cups confectioners' sugar,
sifted
2–3 tbsp freshly squeezed orange
juice
¼ cup mixed colored glacé cherries,
chopped
2½ tbsp mixed citrus peel,
chopped

STORING
This cake can be kept for up to two
days in an airtight container.

For variation, bake the cake in a 7 inch round cake pan, if wished. Use the same quantities of ingredients and follow the method as described here. Decorate with crystallized fruits instead of the glacé cherries and mixed citrus peel.

1 Preheat the oven to 350°F. Grease a 2 lb loaf pan, line the base and sides with waxed paper and then grease the paper.

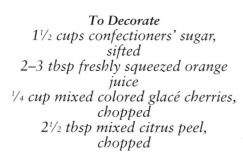

2 ▲ Place the cherries, preserved ginger and mixed citrus peel in a plastic bag with 1 tbsp of the self-rising flour and shake to coat evenly. Sift the remaining flours and cornstarch into a small bowl.

3 ▲ Place the butter and sugar in a mixing bowl and beat until light and fluffy. Beat in the eggs, one at a time, until evenly blended. Fold in the sifted flours with the orange zest, then stir in the dried fruit.

4 ▲ Transfer the cake mixture to the prepared pan and bake in the center of the oven for about 1¼ hours, or until a skewer inserted into the center of the cake comes out clean. Leave the cake in the pan for about 5 minutes, then turn out on to a wire rack, peel off the lining paper and leave to cool completely.

5 ▲ To decorate the cake, place the confectioners' sugar in a mixing bowl. Stir in the orange juice and mix until smooth. Drizzle the icing over the cake. Mix together the chopped glacé cherries and mixed citrus peel in a small bowl, then use to decorate the cake. Allow the icing to set before serving.

Strawberry Cream Gâteau

Fresh raspberries also work well for this recipe.

INGREDIENTS
Serves 8–10
2 egg yolks
4 large eggs
finely grated zest of 1 lemon
½ cup superfine sugar
1 cup flour, sifted
½ cup butter, melted

For the Strawberry Cream
1½ cups fresh strawberries,
washed, dried and hulled
1¼ cups heavy cream
½ cup confectioners' sugar
1 tbsp strawberry liqueur or Kirsch

STORING
This cake can be kept for up to two days in the refrigerator.

1 Preheat the oven to 300°F. Grease an 8 inch round cake pan, line the base with waxed paper and then grease the paper.

2 Place the eggs yolks, egg, lemon zest and sugar in a mixing bowl and beat with electric beaters for about 10 minutes or until thick and pale. Add the flour and melted butter. Beat for a further minute, then transfer to the prepared cake pan.

3 ▲ Bake in the center of the oven for 30–35 minutes or until a skewer inserted into the center of the cake comes out clean. Turn out on to a wire rack, peel off the lining paper and leave to cool completely.

4 ▲ To make the strawberry cream, place all but one of the strawberries in a food processor and purée until smooth. Place the heavy cream in a bowl and whip until it holds peaks. Fold the purée into the cream with the confectioners' sugar and liqueur.

5 ▲ Place the cooled cake on a plate and spread the strawberry cream evenly over the top and sides, making swirls for an attractive finish. Decorate with the sliced reserved strawberry.

*S*imnel Cake

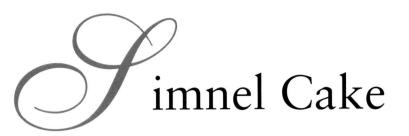

A traditional cake for Easter.

INGREDIENTS
Serves 10–12
1 cup butter, softened
1 cup superfine sugar
4 large eggs, beaten
3 cups mixed dried fruit
such as apricots or prunes
½ cup glacé cherries
3 tbsp sherry (optional)
2½ cups flour, sifted
3 tsp ground allspice
1 tsp baking powder
1½ lb yellow marzipan
1 egg yolk, beaten
ribbons and sugared eggs, to
decorate

STORING
This cake can be kept for up to two weeks in an airtight container.

1 Preheat the oven to 325°F. Lightly grease a deep 8 in round cake pan, line with a double thickness of waxed paper and grease the paper.

2 Place the butter and sugar in a large mixing bowl and beat until light and fluffy. Gradually beat in the eggs. Stir in the dried fruit, glacé cherries and sherry, if using.

3 ▲ Sift together the flour, allspice and baking powder, then fold into the cake mixture. Set aside.

4 ▲ Cut off half of the marzipan and roll out on a work surface dusted with confectioners' sugar to an 8 inch round. Spoon half of the cake mixture into the prepared pan and smooth the surface with the back of a spoon. Place the marzipan round on top, then add the other half of the cake mixture and smooth the surface.

5 Bake in the center of the oven for about 2½ hours or until golden and springy to the touch. Leave the cake in the pan for about 15 minutes, then turn out on to a wire rack, peel off the lining paper and leave to cool completely.

6 ▲ Roll out the other half of the marzipan to a round to fit on top of the cooled cake. Brush the top of the cake with a little of the egg yolk and position the marzipan round on top. Flute the edges of the marzipan and, if liked, make a decorative pattern on top with a fork. Brush with more egg yolk.

7 Put the cake on a baking sheet and place under a broiler for 5 minutes or until the top is lightly browned. Leave to cool before decorating with ribbons and sugared eggs.

Black Forest Gâteau

A perfect gâteau for a special occasion tea party, or for serving as a sumptuous dessert at a dinner party.

INGREDIENTS
Serves 10–12
5 large eggs
³/₄ cup superfine sugar
¹/₂ cup flour, sifted
¹/₃ cup cocoa powder, sifted
6 tbsp butter, melted

For the Filling
5–6 tbsp Kirsch
2¹/₂ cups heavy cream
1 x 15 oz can black cherries,
drained, pitted and chopped

To Decorate
8 x 1 oz squares plain chocolate
15–20 fresh cherries, preferably
with stems
sifted confectioners' sugar (optional)

STORING
This cake is not suitable for storing.

1 Preheat the oven to 350°F. Grease two deep 8 inch round cake pans, line the bases with waxed paper and grease the paper.

2 ▲ Place the eggs and sugar in a large mixing bowl and beat with electric beaters for about 10 minutes or until the mixture is thick and pale.

3 Sift together the flour and cocoa powder, then sift again into the whisked mixture. Fold in very gently, then slowly trickle in the melted butter and continue to fold in gently.

4 Divide the mixture between the pans and smooth the surfaces. Bake in the center of the oven for about 30 minutes, or until springy to the touch. Leave in the pans for about 5 minutes, then turn out on to a wire rack, peel off the lining paper and leave to cool.

5 ▲ Cut each cake in half horizontally and lay on a work surface. Sprinkle the four layers with the Kirsch.

6 ▲ In a large bowl, whip the cream until it holds soft peaks. Transfer two-thirds of the cream to another bowl and stir in the chopped cherries. Place a layer of cake on a serving plate or cake board and spread over one-third of the filling. Top with another layer of cake and continue layering, finishing with a layer of cake.

7 Use the remaining whipped cream to cover the top and sides of the gâteau, spreading it evenly with a knife.

8 To decorate the gâteau, melt the chocolate in a bowl over a pan of hot water, or in a double boiler. Spread the chocolate out on to a plastic chopping board and allow to set.

9 ▲ Using a long, sharp knife, scrape along the surface of the melted chocolate to make thin shavings and use these to cover the sides of the cake and to decorate the top. Finish by arranging the cherries on top of the gâteau. Dust with confectioners' sugar, if wished.

Tip

If liked, the cherries can be coated or half-coated in chocolate before arranging on the cake. To do this, reserve 2–3 tbsp of the melted chocolate and dip the cherries into it. Allow the dipped cherries to set on waxed paper.

Vegan Chocolate Gâteau

It isn't often that vegans can indulge in a slice of chocolate cake, and this one tastes so delicious, they'll all be back for more!

INGREDIENTS
Serves 8–10
2½ cups self-rising whole wheat flour
⅓ cup cocoa powder
3 tsp baking powder
1¼ cups superfine sugar
few drops of vanilla extract
9 tbsp sunflower oil
1½ cups water
sifted cocoa powder, to decorate
¼ cup chopped nuts, to decorate

For the Chocolate Fudge
¼ cup soy margarine
3 tbsp water
2⅓ cups confectioners' sugar
2 tbsp cocoa powder
1–2 tbsp hot water

STORING
This cake can be kept for up to two days in the refrigerator.

1 Preheat the oven to 325°F. Grease a deep 8 inch round cake pan, line the base and sides with waxed paper and grease the paper.

2 Sift the flour, cocoa powder and baking powder into a large mixing bowl. Add the superfine sugar and vanilla extract, then gradually beat in the sunflower oil and water to make a smooth batter.

3 Pour the cake mixture into the prepared pan and smooth the surface with the back of a spoon.

4 ▲ Bake in the center of the oven for about 45 minutes or until a skewer inserted into the center of the cake comes out clean. Leave in the pan for about 5 minutes, then turn out on to a wire rack, peel off the lining paper and leave to cool. Cut the cake in half.

5 ▲ To make the chocolate fudge, place the margarine and water in a pan and heat gently until the margarine has melted. Remove from the heat and add the sifted confectioners' sugar and cocoa powder, beating until smooth and shiny. Allow to cool until firm enough to spread and pipe.

6 ▲ Place the bottom layer of cake on a serving plate and spread over two-thirds of the chocolate fudge mixture. Top with the other layer of cake. Fit a piping bag with a star nozzle, fill with the remaining chocolate fudge and pipe stars over the cake. Sprinkle with cocoa powder and chopped nuts.

Exotic Celebration Gâteau

Use any tropical fruits you can find to make a spectacular display of colors and tastes.

INGREDIENTS
Serves 8–10
¾ cup butter, softened
¾ cup superfine sugar
3 large eggs, beaten
2¼ cups self-rising flour
2–3 tbsp milk
6–8 tbsp light rum
scant 2 cups heavy or whipping cream
¼ cup confectioners' sugar, sifted

To Decorate
1 lb mixed fresh exotic and soft fruits, such as figs, red currants, star fruit, kiwi fruit, etc.
6 tbsp apricot jam, warmed and sieved
2 tbsp warm water
sifted confectioners' sugar

STORING
This cake will keep for up to two days in the refrigerator.

1 Preheat the oven to 375°F. Lightly grease and flour a deep 8 inch ring mold.

2 ▲ Place the butter and sugar in a mixing bowl and beat until light and fluffy. Gradually beat in the eggs, then fold in the flour with the milk.

3 Spoon the cake mixture into the prepared pan and smooth the surface. Bake in the center of the oven for about 45 minutes, or until a skewer inserted into the center of the cake comes out clean. Turn out on to a wire rack and leave to cool completely.

4 ▲ Place the cake on a serving plate, then use a thin skewer to make holes randomly over the cake. Drizzle over the rum and allow to soak in.

5 ▲ Place the cream and confectioners' sugar in a mixing bowl and beat with electric beaters until the mixture holds soft peaks. Spread all over the top and sides of the cake.

6 Arrange the fruits attractively in the hollow center of the cake, allowing the fruits to overhang the edges a little. Mix together the apricot jam and water, then use to brush evenly over the fruit. Sift over a little confectioners' sugar.

Chocolate Chestnut Roulade

A traditional version of the classic Bûche de Nöel, the famous and delicious French Christmas gâteau.

INGREDIENTS
Serves 6–8
8 x 1 oz squares plain chocolate
2 x 1 oz squares white chocolate
4 large eggs, separated
½ cup superfine sugar, plus extra for dredging

For the Chestnut Filling
⅔ cup heavy cream
1 x 8 oz can chestnut purée
4–5 tbsp confectioners' sugar, plus extra for dredging
1–2 tbsp brandy

STORING
This cake can be kept for up to two days in the refrigerator.

1 Preheat the oven to 350°F. Grease a 9 x 13 inch jelly roll pan, line with waxed paper and grease the paper.

2 Place 2 oz of the plain chocolate and the white chocolate in two bowls and set over saucepans of hot water. Stir until melted.

3 ▲ Pour the plain chocolate on to a plastic chopping board and spread out evenly. When just set, do the same with the white chocolate. Leave to set.

4 To make the chocolate curls, hold a long, sharp knife at a 45° angle to the chocolate and push it along the chocolate, turning the knife in a circular motion. Carefully place the plain and white chocolate curls on a baking sheet lined with waxed paper and set aside until needed.

5 ▲ Place the remaining plain chocolate in another bowl set over a saucepan of hot water and stir until melted. Set aside. Place the egg yolks and superfine sugar in a mixing bowl and beat with electric beaters until thick and pale. Stir in the chocolate.

6 Whisk the egg whites in a clean dry bowl, until they hold stiff peaks. Fold into the chocolate mixture and then turn into the prepared pan. Bake in the center of the oven for 15–20 minutes, or until risen and firm. Place on a wire rack, cover with a just-damp cloth and leave to cool completely.

7 Place a sheet of waxed paper on the work surface and sprinkle with a little superfine sugar. Turn the roulade out on to the waxed paper. Peel away the lining paper and trim the edges of the roulade. Cover again with a just-damp cloth.

8 To make the filling, whip the heavy cream in a mixing bowl, until it holds soft peaks.

9 ▲ Place the chestnut purée and confectioners' sugar in a clean bowl. Add the brandy and beat until smooth and evenly combined, then fold in the whipped cream.

10 ▲ Spread the mixture over the roulade, leaving a little border at the top edge. Roll up the roulade, using the waxed paper to help, and transfer it to a serving plate. Top with the chocolate curls and sprinkle with sifted confectioners' sugar, to serve.

Special Occasion Cakes

Here you will find inspired ideas for christenings, Christmas, Halloween, Easter, birthdays and Valentine's Day. Employing an imaginative variety of decorating techniques, the recipes range from a sumptuous chocolate-iced anniversary cake to a wonderful royal-iced wedding extravaganza.

Daisy Christening Cake

A ring of molded daisies sets off this pretty pink christening cake. It can be made in easy stages, giving time for the various icings to dry before adding the next layer.

INGREDIENTS
Serves 20–25
8 inch round Rich Fruit Cake
3 tbsp apricot jam, warmed and sieved
1½ lb marzipan
2 lb/1⅓ x quantity Royal Icing
4 oz/⅓ quantity Sugarpaste Icing
pink and yellow food colorings

MATERIALS AND EQUIPMENT
10 inch round cake board
2 inch fluted cutter
wooden toothpick
2 waxed paper piping bags
No 42 nozzle
pink and white ribbons

STORING
This cake can be kept for up to three months in an airtight container.

1 Brush the cake with the apricot jam. Roll out the marzipan on a work surface lightly dusted with confectioners' sugar and use to cover the cake. Leave to dry for 12 hours.

2 Secure the cake to the cake board with a little of the icing. Color three-quarters of the icing pink. Flat ice the cake with three or four layers of smooth icing, using the white icing for the top and the pink for the sides. Allow each layer to dry overnight before applying the next. Set aside a little of both icings in airtight containers, to decorate the cake.

3 Meanwhile, make the daisies. You will need about 28. For each daisy cut off a small piece of sugarpaste icing. Dust your fingers with a little cornstarch to prevent sticking.

4 ▲ Shape the icing with your fingers to look like a golf tee, with a stem and a thin, flat, round top.

5 ▲ Using scissors, make small cuts all the way around the edge of the daisy. Carefully curl the cut edges slightly in different directions. Place the daisies on a sheet of waxed paper to dry.

6 ▲ When dry, trim the stems and paint the edges with pink and the centers with yellow food coloring.

7 ▲ To make the plaque, roll out the remaining sugarpaste icing on a work surface lightly dusted with confectioners' sugar and cut out a circle with the fluted cutter. Position the end of a wooden toothpick over ¼ inch of the outer edge of the circle. Roll the toothpick firmly back and forth around the edge with your finger until the edge becomes thinner and begins to frill. Continue until the edge of the plaque is completely frilled. Place on a sheet of waxed paper to dry, then paint the name in the center of the plaque and the edges with pink food coloring.

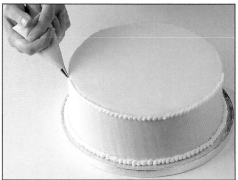

8 ▲ Fit a paper piping bag with the nozzle and pipe a twisted rope around the top and bottom edges of the cake with the remaining white royal icing. Wash the nozzle, fit it in a fresh paper piping bag and pipe a row of stars around the top of the cake with the remaining pink icing.

9 Secure the plaque to the center of the cake with a little royal icing. Arrange the daisies on the cake, also securing with the icing, and decorate with the ribbons.

Rose Blossom Wedding Cake

The traditional white wedding cake, with its classic lines and elegant piping, is still a favorite choice for many brides and grooms.

INGREDIENTS
Serves 80
*9 inch square Rich Fruit Cake
6 inch square Rich Fruit Cake
7 tbsp apricot jam, warmed and
sieved
3½ lb marzipan
3½ lb/2⅓ x quantity Royal Icing,
to coat
1½ lb/1 quantity Royal Icing,
to pipe
pink and green food colorings*

MATERIALS AND EQUIPMENT
*11 inch square cake board
8 inch square cake board
No 1 writing and No 42 nozzles
several waxed paper piping bags
thin pink ribbon
8 pink bows
3–4 cake pillars
about 12 miniature roses
few fern sprigs*

STORING
*The finished cake can be kept for up
to three months in an airtight
container.*

1 Brush the cakes with the apricot jam and cover with marzipan, allowing 1 lb marzipan for the 6 inch cake and the remainder for the 9 inch cake. Place the cakes on the cake boards and leave to dry for 12 hours.

2 Make the royal icing for coating the cake. Secure the cakes to the cake boards with a little of the icing. Flat ice the cakes with three or four layers of smooth icing, allowing each layer to dry overnight before applying the next. The royal icing should be very dry before assembling the cake, so it can be made to this stage and stored in cardboard cake boxes for several days.

3 Make the royal icing for piping, and color a small amount pale pink and another small portion pale green. To make the piped sugar pieces, draw the double-triangle design on a piece of waxed paper several times. You will need 40 pieces, but make extra in case of breakages. Tape the paper to a baking sheet or flat board and secure a piece of parchment paper over the top. Tape it down at the corners.

4 ▲ Fit a piping bag with a No 1 writing nozzle. Half-fill with white royal icing and fold over the top to seal. Pipe over each design, carefully following the outlines with a continuous thread of icing. Spoon a little of the pink icing and a little of the green icing into separate paper piping bags fitted with No 1 writing nozzles. Pipe pink dots on the corners of the top triangle in each design and green on the corners of the bottom triangle in each design. Leave to dry for at least two hours.

5 Mark four triangles on the top and side of each cake with a pin. Work from the center of each side, so each triangle is 2½ inches wide at the base and 1½ inches high on the smaller cake, and 3 inches wide at the base and 2 inches high on the larger cake. Fit a paper piping bag with a clean No 1 writing nozzle and half-fill with some of the white icing. Using the pin marks as a guide, pipe double lines to outline the triangles.

6 ▲ Using the same nozzle, pipe cornelli inside all the triangles.

7 ▲ Fit a piping bag with a No 42 nozzle and half-fill with white icing. Pipe shells around the top and bottom edges of each cake, but not within the triangles.

8 Using the piping bags fitted with No 1 writing nozzles and filled with pink and green icing, pipe dots on the corners of each cake.

9 ▲ Remove the piped sugar pieces from the paper by carefully turning it back and lifting off each piece with a spatula. Secure them to the cake and cake board with a little icing.

10 Decorate the cake with the ribbon and bows. Just before serving, assemble the cake with the cake pillars and decorate with the roses and fern sprigs.

*B*luebird Bon Voyage Cake

This cake is sure to see someone off on an exciting journey in a very special way.

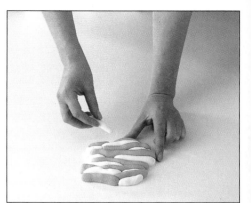

INGREDIENTS
Serves 12–15
*1 lb/²⁄₃ quantity Royal Icing
blue food coloring
1³⁄₄ lb/2¹⁄₃ x quantity Sugarpaste
Icing
8 inch round Madeira Cake
1 quantity Butter Icing
3 tbsp apricot jam, warmed and
sieved
silver balls*

MATERIALS AND EQUIPMENT
*10 inch round cake board
waxed paper piping bags
No 1 writing nozzle
thin pale blue ribbon*

STORING
The finished cake can be kept for up to one week in an airtight container.

1 Make up the royal icing, keeping about two-thirds softer for filling in, and the rest stiffer for the outlines and further piping. Color the softer icing blue. Cover the icings and leave them overnight. Stir before using.

2 ▲ On waxed paper, draw the birds several times in two sizes. Tape the paper to a baking sheet with masking tape, then secure a piece of parchment paper over the top.

3 ▲ Fit a paper piping bag with a No 1 writing nozzle and spoon in some of the stiffer icing for piping the outlines. Pipe over the outlines of the birds with a continuous thread of icing.

4 ▲ Half-fill a fresh paper piping bag with the blue icing. Cut the pointed end off the bag in a straight line. Do not make the opening too large or the icing will flow too quickly. Pipe the icing into the outlines to fill, working from the outlines into the center. Do not touch the outlines or they may break. To prevent air bubbles, keep the end of the bag in the icing. The icing should look overfilled and rounded, as it will shrink slightly as it dries.

5 Working quickly, brush through the icing to fill in any gaps and to ensure it goes right to the outlines. If any air bubbles appear, smooth them out or burst with a pin. Leave the run-outs on the paper for two days to dry.

6 ▲ Color two-thirds of the sugar-paste icing blue and leave the rest white. Form the icing into small rolls and place them together on a work surface lightly dusted with confectioners' sugar, alternating the colors. Form into a round and lightly knead together until the icing is marbled. Do not over-knead or you will lose the effect. Cut off about one-quarter of the sugarpaste icing, wrap in plastic wrap and set aside.

7 Cut the cake horizontally into three even layers and sandwich together with the butter icing. Brush with the apricot jam. Roll out the marbled sugarpaste icing and use it to cover the cake. Roll out the reserved sugarpaste icing to a 10 inch circle and use it to cover the cake board.

8 ▲ Position the cake to one edge of the board. Fit a piping bag with the writing nozzle and half-fill with the remaining stiffer royal icing. Pipe a wavy line all around the edge of the cake board. Working quickly before the icing dries, position the silver balls so they are evenly spaced in the icing.

9 Remove the birds from the waxed paper using a spatula and secure them to the cake with a little royal icing. Pipe a bead of white icing on each for the eye and place a silver ball in the center. Drape the ribbon between the birds' beaks, securing it with a little icing.

Fudge-frosted Starry Roll

Whether it's a birthday or another occasion you are wanting to celebrate, this sumptuous looking cake is sure to please.

INGREDIENTS
Serves 8
1 quantity Jelly Roll mix
½ quantity chocolate-flavor Butter Icing
2 x 1 oz squares white chocolate
2 x 1 oz squares plain chocolate
1½ x quantity Fudge Frosting

MATERIALS AND EQUIPMENT
9 x 13 inch jelly roll pan
small star cutter
several waxed paper piping bags
No 19 star nozzle

STORING
This cake can be kept for up to two days in an airtight container, stored in the refrigerator.

1 Preheat the oven to 350°F. Grease the pan, line the base with waxed paper and grease the paper. Spoon in the cake mixture and gently smooth the surface. Bake for 12–15 minutes, or until springy to the touch.

2 Turn out on to a sheet of waxed paper lightly sprinkled with superfine sugar, peel off the lining paper and roll up the jelly roll, leaving the lining paper inside. When cold, unroll carefully, remove the paper and spread the cake with the butter icing. Re-roll and set aside on a sheet of waxed paper on a wire rack.

3 ▲ To make the chocolate decorations, cover a board with parchment paper and tape it down at each corner. Melt the white chocolate, then pour on to the parchment paper. Spread the chocolate evenly with a spatula and allow to stand until the surface is firm enough to cut, but not so hard that it will break. It should no longer feel sticky when touched with your finger. Press a small star cutter firmly through the chocolate and lift off the paper with a spatula. Set aside.

4 ▲ Melt the plain chocolate and allow to cool slightly. Cover a rolling pin with parchment paper and attach it with tape. Fill a paper piping bag with the chocolate and cut a small piece off the pointed end in a straight line. Pipe lines of chocolate backwards and forwards over the parchment paper, to the size you choose. Make at least nine curls so you have extra in case of breakages. Leave the chocolate lace curls to set in a cool place, then carefully peel off the paper.

5 ▲ Make the fudge frosting. When cool enough to spread, cover the jelly roll with about two-thirds of it, making swirls with a spatula.

6 ▲ Fit a fresh paper piping bag with the No 19 star nozzle and spoon in the remaining frosting. Pipe diagonal lines, like a twisted rope, on either side of the roll and across both ends.

7 ▲ Position the lace curls in the icing, and arrange the stars. Transfer the cake to a serving plate and decorate with more stars.

*L*ucky Horseshoe

This horseshoe-shaped cake, made to wish "good luck," is made from a round cake and the horseshoe shape is then cut out.

INGREDIENTS
Serves 30–35
10 inch Rich Fruit Cake
4 tbsp apricot jam, warmed and sieved
1¾ lb marzipan
2¼ lb/3 x quantity Sugarpaste Icing
peach and blue food colorings
silver balls
4 oz/⅙ quantity Royal Icing

MATERIALS AND EQUIPMENT
11–12 inch round cake board
crimping tool
large blossom cutter
small blossom cutter
pale blue ribbon, ⅛ in wide

STORING
The cake can be kept for up to three months in an airtight container.

1 Draw a horseshoe shape on a sheet of waxed paper. Cut this shape out of the cake, using the template as a guide. Brush the cake with the apricot jam. Roll out 12 oz of the marzipan to a 10 inch circle on a work surface lightly dusted with confectioners' sugar. Using the template as a guide, cut out the shape and cover the top of the cake with the marzipan. Reserve the trimmings for the inside of the ring.

2 Measure the circumference of the cake as far as the openings of the horseshoe and the height of the side with string. Take the remaining marzipan and roll out for the side, using the string measurement as a guide. Use to cover the side. Using the same method and the reserved trimmings, cover the inside of the horseshoe. Position the cake on the board and leave to dry for 12 hours.

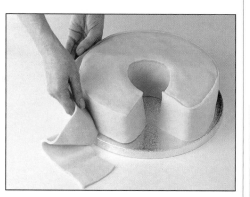

3 ▲ Color 1¾ lb of the sugarpaste icing peach. Brush the marzipan lightly with a little water and cover the cake with the sugarpaste icing in the same way as described for the marzipan, covering first the top, then the side, and finally the inside of the horseshoe shape.

4 Using a crimping tool dipped in cornstarch, carefully crimp the top edge of the cake.

5 Draw and measure the design for the ribbon insertion on the horseshoe template. Cut 13 pieces of pale blue ribbon fractionally longer than the size of each slit.

6 ▲ Place the template on the cake, securing with pins if necessary, and cut through the drawn lines into the icing with a scalpel to make slits for the ribbon. Remove the template.

7 ▲ With the aid of a pointed tool, insert one end of the ribbon into the first slit and the other end into the second slit. Leave a space and repeat, filling all the slits with the pieces of ribbon. Leave to dry for 12 hours.

8 ▲ Draw a small horseshoe shape on a piece of cardboard and cut out. Take the remaining sugarpaste icing and color one-half pale blue and leave the other half white. Roll out the blue icing on a lightly dusted work surface. Using the cardboard template as a guide, cut out nine shapes. Mark small lines around the center of each horseshoe with the knife. Cut out 12 large and 15 small blossoms with the blossom cutters, then press a silver ball into the centers of the larger blossoms. Leave them to dry on waxed paper. Repeat with the white icing.

9 Decorate the cake with the ribbon. Arrange the horseshoes and blossoms on the cake and board, securing with a little royal icing.

*T*ip

Save the discarded section of the round cake to use in the Truffle Mix, if wished. Horseshoe-shaped pans can be purchased or rented from cake decorating specialists.

Christmas Tree Cake

No piping is involved in this bright and colorful Christmas tree cake, making it a good choice for all the family to help decorate.

INGREDIENTS
Serves 20–25
8 inch round Rich Fruit Cake
3 tbsp apricot jam, warmed and sieved
2 lb marzipan
green, red, yellow and purple food colorings
8 oz/⅓ quantity Royal Icing
silver balls

MATERIALS AND EQUIPMENT
10 inch round cake board

STORING
The finished cake can be kept for up to three months in an airtight container.

1 Brush the cake with the apricot jam. Color 1½ lb of the marzipan green. Roll out the green marzipan on a work surface lightly dusted with confectioners' sugar and use it to cover the cake. Leave to dry for 12 hours.

2 ▲ Make the royal icing. Secure the cake to the cake board with a little of the icing. Spread the icing evenly on the side of the cake to cover just half way up. Starting at the bottom of the cake, press the flat side of a spatula into the icing, then pull away sharply to form a peak. Repeat until the iced area is covered with peaks.

3 ▲ Draw three Christmas tree shapes in different sizes on to a piece of cardboard and cut out. Take half of the remaining marzipan and color it a slightly deeper shade of green than the top. Using the cardboard templates as a guide, cut out three Christmas tree shapes. Arrange the trees on top of the cake.

4 ▲ Divide the remaining marzipan into three portions and color it red, yellow and purple. Use a little of the marzipan to make five 3 inch rolls from each color. Loop the colored lengths alternately around the top edge of the cake, pressing on to the top to secure them firmly.

5 ▲ Make small balls from red marzipan and press on to the end of each loop.

6 ▲ Use the remaining marzipan to make the tree decorations. Roll the red marzipan into a thin rope and cut into eight 1 inch lengths for the candles. Shape eight flames from the yellow icing and stick on the end of each candle. Mold 11 small balls from the purple icing and press a silver ball into the center of each.

7 Arrange the candles and balls on the trees, securing them with a little water if necessary.

Halloween Pumpkin Patch

*Pumpkins have sprung up all over this orange and chocolate cake,
making it the ideal design to celebrate Halloween.*

INGREDIENTS
Serves 12–15
*2 x quantity chocolate-flavor
Quick-Mix Sponge Cake mix
6 oz/2 x quantity Sugarpaste Icing
orange and brown food colorings
2 x quantity orange-flavor Butter
Icing
chocolate chips
angelica*

MATERIALS AND EQUIPMENT
*2 x 8 inch round cake pans
9 inch round cake board
serrated scraper
waxed paper piping bag
No 7 writing nozzle*

STORING
*This cake can be kept for up to
three days in the refrigerator.*

1 Preheat the oven to 325°F. Lightly grease the cake pans, line the bases with waxed paper and then grease the paper.

2 Divide the mixture between the pans and smooth the surfaces. Bake for 20–30 minutes or until firm to the touch. Turn out on to a wire rack, peel off the lining paper and leave to cool.

3 ▲ To make the pumpkins, color a very small piece of the sugarpaste icing brown, and the rest orange. Dust your fingers with a little cornstarch. Shape small balls of the orange icing the size of walnuts and some a bit smaller. Make the ridges with a wooden toothpick. Make the stems from the brown icing and press into the top of each pumpkin, securing with a little water. Paint highlights on each pumpkin with orange food coloring. Leave to dry on waxed paper.

4 Cut each cake in half horizontally. Use one-quarter of the butter icing to sandwich the cakes together. Place the cake on the cake board. Use about two-thirds of the remaining icing to coat the top and sides of the cake.

5 Texture the cake sides with a serrated scraper. Decorate the top with the same scraper, moving the scraper sideways to make undulations and a ridged spiral pattern in a slight fan shape. The texturing should resemble a ploughed field.

6 ▲ Fit a paper piping bag with the writing nozzle and spoon in the remaining butter icing. Pipe a twisted rope pattern around the top and bottom edges of the cake.

7 Decorate the piped pattern with chocolate chips.

8 ▲ Cut the angelica into diamond shapes and arrange on the cake with the pumpkins.

Easter Egg Nest Cake

Celebrate Easter with a fresh-tasting lemon sponge cake, colorfully adorned with marzipan nests and chocolate eggs.

INGREDIENTS
Serves 10
1 quantity lemon-flavor Quick-Mix
Sponge Cake mix
1 quantity lemon-flavor
Butter Icing
8 oz marzipan
pink, green and purple food
colorings
foil-wrapped chocolate eggs

MATERIALS AND EQUIPMENT
8 inch ring mold
10 inch cake board

STORING
This cake can be kept for up to three days in an airtight container, stored in the refrigerator.

1 Preheat the oven to 325°F. Grease and flour the ring mold. Spoon the cake mixture into the mold and smooth the surface. Bake in the center of the oven for about 25 minutes, or until golden in color and firm to the touch. Turn out on to a wire rack and leave to cool completely.

2 ▲ Cut the cake in half horizontally and sandwich together with about one-third of the butter icing. Position the cake on the cake board. Spread the remaining icing over the outside of the cake to cover completely.

3 Smooth the top of the cake with a spatula and swirl the icing around the side of the cake.

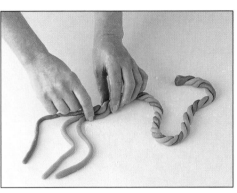

4 ▲ To make the marzipan braids, divide the marzipan into three portions and color it pink, green and purple. Cut each portion in half. Using one-half of each of the colors, roll each one out with your fingers on a work surface lightly dusted with confectioners' sugar to make a thin sausage shape long enough to go around the bottom edge of the cake. Pinch the ends together at the top, then twist the individual strands into a rope. Pinch the other ends to seal neatly.

5 ▲ Place the rope on the cake board around the bottom edge of the cake.

6 To make the nests, take the remaining portions of colored marzipan and divide each color into five. Roll each piece into a rope about 6½ inches long. Take a rope of each color, pinch the ends together, twist to form a multi-colored rope and pinch the other ends. Form the rope into a circle and then repeat the process to make the remaining four nests.

7 ▲ Arrange the nests so they are evenly spaced on the top of the cake and place several chocolate eggs in the middle of each.

Cloth of Roses Cake

This cake says "congratulations" for whatever reason – passing an exam, getting a new job, getting engaged, or for just achieving a lifelong ambition.

INGREDIENTS
Serves 20–25
8 inch round Light Fruit Cake
3 tbsp apricot jam, warmed and sieved
1½ lb marzipan
2 lb/2⅔ x quantity Sugarpaste Icing
yellow, orange and green food colorings
4oz/⅙ quantity Royal Icing

MATERIALS AND EQUIPMENT
10 inch cake board
2¾ inch plain cutter
petal cutter
thin yellow ribbon

STORING
The finished cake can be kept for up to four weeks in an airtight container.

1 Brush the cake with the warmed apricot jam. Roll out the marzipan on a work surface lightly dusted with confectioners' sugar and cover the cake. Leave for 12 hours.

2 Cut off 1½ lb of the sugarpaste icing and divide it in half. Color one-half very pale yellow and the other very pale orange. Wrap separately in plastic wrap and set aside.

3 Cut out a template for the orange icing from waxed paper, as follows. Draw a 10 inch circle using the cake board as a guide. Using the plain cutter, draw half circles 1 inch wide all around the outside of the large circle. Cut out the template.

4 Roll out the yellow sugarpaste icing on a work surface lightly dusted with confectioners' sugar to the same length and height as the side of the cake. Brush the side of the cake with a little water and cover with the sugarpaste icing. Position the cake on the cake board.

5 ▲ Roll out the orange sugarpaste icing to about a 12 inch circle. Place the template on the icing and cut out the scalloped shape.

6 ▲ Brush the top of the cake with water and cover with the orange icing so the scallops fall just over the edge. Bend them slightly to look like a cloth. Leave to dry overnight.

7 Meanwhile make the roses and leaves. Cut off about three-quarters of the remaining sugarpaste icing and divide into four portions. (Wrap the other piece in plastic wrap and reserve for the leaves.) Color the four portions pale yellow, deep yellow, orange, and marbled yellow and orange.

8 ▲ For each rose, dust your fingers with cornstarch, take a small ball of colored icing and form into a cone shape. For each petal, take a small piece of icing and work it with your fingers into a petal shape which is slightly thicker at the base. Wrap the petal around the cone so it sits above the top of it, pressing together to stick. Curl the ends of the petal back. Mold the next petal and attach so it just overlaps the first one. Curl the ends back. Repeat with several more petals, making them slightly larger each time. Cut off the base so the rose will stand on the cake. Make about 18 roses. Leave to dry on waxed paper.

9 ▲ Color the reserved piece of sugarpaste icing green for the leaves. Roll out thinly and cut out leaves with a petal cutter. Make about 24 leaves. Leave to dry on waxed paper.

10 Arrange the leaves and roses, securing with a little royal icing. Decorate the cake with the ribbon.

Birthday Present

Here is a birthday cake that is all wrapped up and ready to eat. The pattern on the iced present can be changed by using different shaped cutters.

INGREDIENTS
Serves 10
6 in square Madeira Cake
³/₄ quantity orange-flavor Butter Icing
3 tbsp apricot jam, warmed and sieved
1 lb/1¹/₃ x quantity Sugarpaste Icing blue, orange and green food colorings

MATERIALS AND EQUIPMENT
7–8 inch square cake board
small round and triangular cocktail cutters

STORING
The finished cake can be kept for up to one week in an airtight container.

1 Cut the cake in half horizontally and sandwich together with the butter icing. Brush the cake with apricot jam. Color three-quarters of the sugarpaste icing blue. Divide the remaining sugarpaste icing in half and color one-half orange and the other half green. Wrap the orange and green sugarpaste separately in plastic wrap and set aside. Roll out the blue icing on a work surface lightly dusted with confectioners' sugar and use it to cover the cake. Position on the cake board.

2 While the sugarpaste covering is still soft, cut out circles and triangles from the blue icing with the cocktail cutters, lifting out the shapes to expose the cake beneath.

3 ▲ Roll out the orange and green icings and use the same cutters to cut out circles and triangles. Replace the exposed holes in the blue icing with the orange and green shapes, easing in to fit. Gather together the orange and green trimmings.

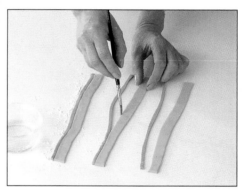

4 ▲ Roll out the orange trimmings and cut three strips about ³/₄ inch wide and long enough to go over each corner of the cake. Roll out the green trimmings and cut three very thin strips the same length as the orange ones. Place the orange and green strips next to each other to give three striped ribbons, and secure the pieces together with a little water.

5 Place one striped ribbon over one corner of the cake, securing with a little water. Place a second strip over the opposite corner.

6 ▲ Cut the remaining ribbon in half. Bend each half to make loops and attach both to one corner of the cake with water to form a loose bow.

Chocolate-iced Anniversary Cake

This cake is special enough to celebrate any wedding anniversary. Tropical fruits and a glossy chocolate icing make it very appealing for all ages.

INGREDIENTS
Serves 12–15
8 inch round Madeira Cake
1½ x quantity chocolate-flavor
Butter Icing
1 quantity Satin Chocolate Icing
chocolate discs
selection of fresh fruits, such as
kiwi, nectarine or peach, apricot,
Cape gooseberries

MATERIALS AND EQUIPMENT
waxed paper piping bag
No 22 star nozzle
thin gold ribbon, about ¼ in wide
florists' wire

STORING
This cake can be kept for up to five days in the refrigerator.

1 Cut the cake into three horizontal layers and sandwich together with about three-quarters of the chocolate butter icing. Place the cake on a wire rack with a baking sheet underneath.

2 ▲ Make the satin chocolate icing and immediately pour over the cake to coat completely. Working quickly, ease the icing gently over the surface of the cake, using a spatula if necessary. Allow to set.

3 ▲ Transfer the cake to a serving plate. Fit a paper piping bag with the star nozzle and spoon in the remaining chocolate butter icing. Pipe scrolls around the top edge of the cake.

4 Cut several chocolate discs into quarters and use to decorate the butter icing.

5 ▲ Prepare the fruit for the top of the cake. Peel and slice the kiwi and cut into quarters, and slice the nectarine or peach, apricot and gooseberries.

6 Arrange the fruit on top of the cake. For each ribbon decoration, make two small loops using the thin gold ribbon. Twist a piece of florists' wire around the ends of the ribbon to secure the loops. Trim the ends of the ribbon. Cut the wire to the length you want and use it to put the loops in position on the cake. Make about seven ribbon decorations. Remove the ribbons and wire before serving.

Golden Wedding Heart Cake

Creamy gold colors, delicate frills and dainty iced blossoms give this cake a special celebratory appeal.

INGREDIENTS
Serves 30
9 inch round Rich Fruit Cake
4 tbsp apricot jam, warmed and sieved
2 lb marzipan
2 lb/2⅔ x quantity Sugarpaste Icing
cream food coloring
4 oz/1/6 quantity Royal Icing

MATERIALS AND EQUIPMENT
11 inch round cake board
crimping tool
small heart-shaped plunger tool
3 inch plain cutter
dual large and small blossom cutter
stamens
frill cutter
foil-wrapped chocolate hearts

STORING
The finished cake can be kept for up to three months in an airtight container.

1 Brush the cake with apricot jam. Roll out the marzipan on a work surface lightly dusted with confectioners' sugar and use it to cover the cake. Leave to dry for 12 hours.

2 Color 1½ lb of the sugarpaste icing very pale cream. Roll out the icing on a work surface lightly dusted with confectioners' sugar. Brush the marzipan with a little water and cover the cake with the sugarpaste icing. Position the cake on the cake board. Using a crimping tool dipped in cornstarch, carefully crimp the top edge of the cake.

3 ▲ Divide the circumference of the top of the cake into eight equal sections, and stick pins in as markers. Use these as a guide to crimp evenly spaced slanting lines going from the top to the bottom edges of the cake. Using the plunger tool, emboss the bottom edge of the cake. Place the plain cutter lightly in the center of the cake and use as a guide to emboss more hearts in a circle around the cutter. Leave the cake to dry for several hours.

4 ▲ Take the remaining sugarpaste icing and color one-half cream and the other half pale cream. Retain half of each color, and wrap the remainder in plastic wrap. Roll out each color evenly and thinly. Dip the end of the blossom cutter in cornstarch and cut out the flower shapes. Make a pin hole in the center of each larger flower as you make it. Leave to dry on a foam pad. When dry, pipe a little royal icing on to a stamen and thread it through the hole of each larger flower. This will hold it in position. Allow to dry.

5 ▲ To make the frills, roll out the two shades of reserved sugarpaste icing thinly. Using the frill cutter, cut out two rings from each color.

6 ▲ Position the end of a wooden toothpick over ¼ inch of the outer edge of the ring. Roll the toothpick firmly back and forth around the edge with your finger until the edge becomes thinner and begins to frill. Continue until the ring is completely frilled. Repeat with remaining rings. Using a sharp knife, cut each ring in half to make two frills. You should have four frills in each shade.

7 ▲ Using a little water, attach the frills in alternate shades next to the crimped lines running down the side of the cake. Crimp the edges of the deeper colored frills.

8 Arrange the blossom flowers on the top and side of the cake, securing with a little royal icing. Before serving, place the chocolate hearts in the center of the cake.

Birthday Bowl of Strawberries

All kinds of fun designs can be painted on cakes with edible food colorings. With this one the strawberry theme is carried on into the molded decorations too, providing a fresh, summery birthday cake.

INGREDIENTS
Serves 20
1 quantity Butter Icing
8 inch petal-shaped Madeira Cake
(make using quantities for an 8 inch round cake)
3 tbsp apricot jam, warmed and sieved
1½ lb/2 x quantity Sugarpaste Icing
pink, red, yellow, green and burgundy food colorings
yellow powdered food coloring

MATERIALS AND EQUIPMENT
10 inch petal-shaped cake board
paint palette or small saucers
thin red and green ribbons

STORING
The finished cake can be kept for up to one week in an airtight container.

1 Color the butter icing pink. Cut the cake into three horizontal layers and sandwich together with the butter icing. Brush the cake with apricot jam. Roll out 1¼ lb of the sugarpaste icing on a work surface lightly dusted with confectioners' sugar and use to cover the cake. Position on the cake board and leave to dry for 12 hours.

2 ▲ To make the strawberries, color three-quarters of the remaining sugarpaste icing red, and equal portions of the rest yellow and green. Dust your fingers with cornstarch to prevent sticking, and mold the red icing into strawberry shapes. Make tiny oval shapes from the yellow icing to represent seeds and lightly press on to the strawberries. Secure with water if necessary. Shape the green icing into small flat circles slightly bigger than the tops of the strawberries. Using scissors, make small cuts all the way round the circles and carefully curl the cut edges slightly. Attach to the tops of the strawberries, securing with a little water. Leave to dry on waxed paper.

3 ▲ Put the red, green, yellow and burgundy food colorings in a palette and water them down slightly. Draw or paint on an outline of the vase with the burgundy color, then fill in the pattern.

4 ▲ Use a little powdered yellow food coloring to add highlights.

5 ▲ Finish painting the design, filling in the strawberries in the bowl and around the edge of the cake.

6 ▲ Decorate the cake with the ribbons. Secure two strawberries to the top of the cake, and arrange the others around the bottom edge.

Children's Novelty Cakes

This section offers fifteen fabulous fantasies for kids of all ages – perfect party cakes and novelties which will form wonderful centerpieces and surprises at any birthday or special event. The fun projects include a pretty Mermaid, a jazzy Jack-in-the-Box, a spooky Halloween Coffin, and an amazing Helicopter Cake.

Ducks on a Pond

A real treat at a children's party. A scrumptious combination of coconut cake, jelly and cream.

INGREDIENTS
Serves 8–10
1 quantity Quick-Mix Sponge Cake mix
2½ cups heavy cream
green, yellow and red food colorings
4 cups shredded coconut
1 x 4½ oz packet of green jelly, made up to the manufacturer's instructions
7 oz/½ quantity Sugarpaste Icing
a few tiny candies
3 oz marzipan
5 pink marshmallows

MATERIALS AND EQUIPMENT
7 inch pie pan
9 inch round cake board
duck-shaped cutter
toothpicks
garlic press

STORING
The finished cake can be refrigerated for up to three days.

1 Preheat the oven to 350°F. Grease the pie pan, line the base with waxed paper and grease the paper. Spoon the cake mixture into the prepared pan and smooth the surface. Bake in the center of the oven for 35–40 minutes or until firm to the touch. Leave the cake in the pan for about 3 minutes, then turn out on to a wire rack, peel off the lining paper and leave to cool completely.

2 ▲ Add a few drops of green food coloring to the heavy cream, and beat until it holds soft peaks. Place the cake on the cake board and spread the cream evenly over the cake.

3 ▲ To make the grassy bank, place the coconut in a bowl and add a few drops of green food coloring diluted with a dash of water. Stir until the coconut is speckled green and white.

4 ▲ Cut up the set jelly into ½ inch pieces. Carefully place the jelly pieces in the center of the cake.

5 To make the ducks, take 3 oz of the sugarpaste icing and color it yellow. Roll out on a work surface lightly dusted with confectioners' sugar until about ¼ inch thick.

6 ▲ Using a duck-shaped cutter, stamp out the ducks, then skewer the bottom of each one with a toothpick. Lay the ducks on a baking sheet and leave them in a warm, dry place to harden.

7 Use the tiny candies, or sugarpaste icing, for the ducks' eyes, securing with a drop of water. Take off a small piece of marzipan, about the size of a hazelnut, then color the remainder green and shape into a frog, using a small, sharp knife to open the mouth and make the feet. Color the reserved piece of marzipan red, shape into the frog's tongue and secure in position with a little water. Use candies or blue and white sugarpaste icing for the eyes. Place the frog on the cake board.

8 To make the grass, color the remaining sugarpaste icing green and push through a garlic press, cutting it off with a small, sharp knife. Place the grass around the pond. To make the flowers, flatten the marshmallows with a rolling pin, then snip the edges with scissors to make the petals. Place the flowers around the pond and put a colored candy in the center of each. The wooden toothpicks must be removed from the ducks before serving.

$\mathcal{D}$ump Truck

*Any large, round cookies will work well for the wheels, and
all sorts of colored candies can go in the truck.*

INGREDIENTS
Serves 8–10
*1½ x quantity Quick-Mix Sponge
Cake mix
6 tbsp apricot jam, warmed and
sieved
2 lb/2²⁄₃ x quantity Sugarpaste Icing
yellow, red and blue food colorings
confectioners' sugar, to dredge
sandwich wafer cookies
4 coconut swirl cookies
4 oz colored candies
2 inch piece blue liquorice stick
raw sugar, for the sand*

MATERIALS AND EQUIPMENT
*2 lb loaf pan
12 x 7 inch cake board
7 x 3 inch piece of cake cardboard,
brushed with apricot jam
small crescent-shaped cutter*

STORING
*The cake can be completed up to
three days in advance and kept in a
cool, dry place.*

1 Preheat the oven to 350°F. Grease the pan, line the base and sides with waxed paper and grease the paper. Spoon the cake mixture into the pan and smooth the surface. Bake in the center of the oven for 40–45 minutes or until a skewer inserted into the center of the cake comes out clean. Turn out on to a wire rack, peel off the lining paper and leave the cake to cool completely.

2 Using a large, sharp knife, cut off the top of the cake to make a flat surface. Then cut off one-third of the cake to make the cabin of the truck.

3 ▲ Take the larger piece of cake, and, with the cut side up, cut a hollow in the center, leaving a ½ inch border. Brush the hollowed cake evenly with apricot jam.

4 ▲ Color 12 oz of the sugarpaste icing yellow and remove a piece about the size of a walnut. Set aside, wrapped in plastic wrap. Roll out the remainder on a work surface lightly dusted with confectioners' sugar until about ¼ inch thick. Use to cover the hollowed-out piece of cake, carefully pressing it into the hollow. Trim the bottom edges and then set aside.

5 Color 12 oz of the sugarpaste icing red. Cut off one-third of this and set aside, wrapped in plastic wrap. Roll out the rest on a work surface dusted with confectioners' sugar until about ¼ inch thick. Use to cover the remaining piece of cake and trim the edges.

6 Take the reserved red icing, break off a piece the size of a walnut and wrap in plastic wrap. Roll out the rest and use to cover the cake cardboard.

7 ▲ Brush the wafers with a little apricot jam and stick them together in two equal piles. Place the piles on the cake board, about 3 inches apart. Place the red-covered cake cardboard on top of the wafers. Place a little of the remaining white sugarpaste icing about half way along the covered cardboard in order to tip the bed part of the truck slightly. Place the bed on top, with the cabin in front. Stand the coconut cookies in position for the wheels.

8 ▲ Roll out the reserved piece of yellow sugarpaste icing to make a 2 x 1 inch rectangle. Color the remaining white sugarpaste icing with blue food coloring and roll out thinly. Use the crescent-shaped cutter to stamp out the eyes. Either make simple ones, or overlay them with white crescent shapes for detail.

9 Roll out the reserved red sugarpaste icing thinly and stamp out a mouth shape with an appropriate cutter. Use a little water to stick the yellow panel on to the front of the truck, then stick on the features in the same way.

10 To finish, fill the bed part of the truck with brightly colored candies and push a piece of colored liquorice into the top of the cabin. Scatter the sugar around the base of the dump truck to resemble sand.

Train Cake

This quick-and-easy train cake is made in a shaped pan, so all you need to do is decorate it!

INGREDIENTS
Serves 8–10
1½ x quantity Quick-Mix Sponge
Cake mix
yellow food coloring
2 x quantity Butter Icing
red liquorice strings
6–8 tbsp colored jimmies
4 liquorice wheels

MATERIALS AND EQUIPMENT
train-shaped cake pan
10 x 15 inch cake board
2 fabric piping bags
small round and small star nozzles
pink and white cotton wool balls

STORING
*The decorated cake should be made
and served on the same day.*

Tip

When applying butter icing to a
cake, it is a good idea to have a
small bowl of very hot water at the
ready to dip your spatula into. This
will ensure that you get a really
smooth finish on the cake.

1 Preheat the oven to 350°F. Grease
and flour the cake pan and stand
firmly on a greased baking sheet.
Grease some strips of foil and press
along the edges of the cake pan
to prevent the cake mixture escaping.
Spoon the cake mixture into the
prepared pan and smooth the surface.
Bake in the center of the oven for 40–
45 minutes or until a skewer inserted
into the center of the cake comes out
clean. Leave the cake to cool in the pan.

2 ▲ Slice off the top surface of the
cake to make it perfectly flat. Run a
knife around the edges of the cake to
release it from the pan, then turn out
the cake and place on the cake board.

3 ▲ Add a few drops of yellow food
coloring to the butter icing and beat
well until evenly blended.

4 ▲ Using a spatula, cover the cake
smoothly with about half of the
butter icing.

5 ▲ Fit a piping bag with a round
nozzle and fill with about one-
quarter of the remaining butter icing.
Pipe a straight border around the edges
of the cake. Repeat the process to make
a double-edged border.

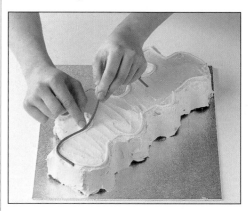

6 ▲ Position the red liquorice strings
around the edge of the cake, on top
of the piped border. Snip the strings
with scissors as you bend them around
the curves on the train.

7 Fit a piping bag with a small star
nozzle and fill with the remaining
butter icing. Pipe small stars evenly over
the top of the cake. Add extra details
to the train with the liquorice, or by
piping, if you like. Use a spatula to
press on the colored jimmies all around
the sides of the cake.

8 Pull a few balls of cotton wool apart
for the steam and stick in position
with a little butter icing. Press the
liquorice wheels in place.

Telephone Cake

A great idea for a first or second birthday, as the telephone is an endless source of amusement for many toddlers.

INGREDIENTS
Serves 8–10
1 quantity chocolate-flavor Quick-Mix Sponge Cake mix
6 tbsp apricot jam, warmed and sieved
1¼ lb/1⅔ x quantity Sugarpaste Icing
1 quantity Butter Icing
red, blue, yellow and green food colorings
black liquorice ribbon

MATERIALS AND EQUIPMENT
7 inch square cake pan
8 inch square cake board
3 waxed paper piping bags
small round cutter

STORING
The iced cake can be kept in a cool, dry place for up to three days.

1 Preheat the oven to 350°F. Grease the pan, line with waxed paper and grease the paper. Spoon the mixture into the pan and smooth the surface. Bake in the center of the oven for 35 – 40 minutes or until firm. Turn out and leave to cool.

2 ▲ Cut off a 1½ inch strip for the receiver. Cut the main body of the telephone in half. Cut about one-quarter off the top half of the main body of the telephone for the receiver rest.

3 ▲ Brush the center of the main cake with apricot jam and reposition the top of the cake, leaving space to replace the receiver rest.

4 ▲ To shape the receiver rest, cut a ½ inch cross out of the center of this portion, then cut away the four end corners. Brush the base with apricot jam and position on the cake.

5 ▲ Brush the top surface of the cake evenly with apricot jam. On a work surface lightly dusted with confectioners' sugar, roll out 12 oz of the sugarpaste icing to a 12 inch square and use to cover the telephone cake. Place the cake on the cake board.

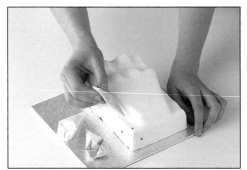

6 ▲ Divide the butter icing into three separate bowls, coloring one red, one blue and one yellow. Fill the piping bags with the colored butter icings and snip the end off each one to make a small hole. Pipe spots in all three colors evenly over the cake.

7 Color 6 oz of the remaining sugarpaste icing green. Cut off about 1 oz and set aside, wrapped in plastic wrap. Brush the receiver piece of cake with a little apricot jam, then roll out the larger piece of green sugarpaste icing and use to cover the receiver. Position the receiver on the cake.

8 Take a small piece of the remaining green sugarpaste icing and roll it into a ball. Stick it on to the side of the receiver with a little water.

9 Roll out the remaining green sugarpaste icing and cut out a flower pot shape, measuring approximately 3 inches across the top. Place this on the front of the telephone, sticking it down with a little water. To make the dial, color the remaining sugarpaste icing red and roll out to a 3 inch round, or stamp it out using a cutter. Use a tiny round cutter to stamp out the finger holes, then position the dial on the cake with a little water. Use any remaining butter cream to pipe in the numbers.

10 To make the telephone cord, twist the piece of liquorice around a pencil until tightly coiled and leave it for about 10 minutes. Carefully remove the pencil, and press one end of the liquorice into the ball of green sugarpaste icing on the receiver and the other end into the back of the cake.

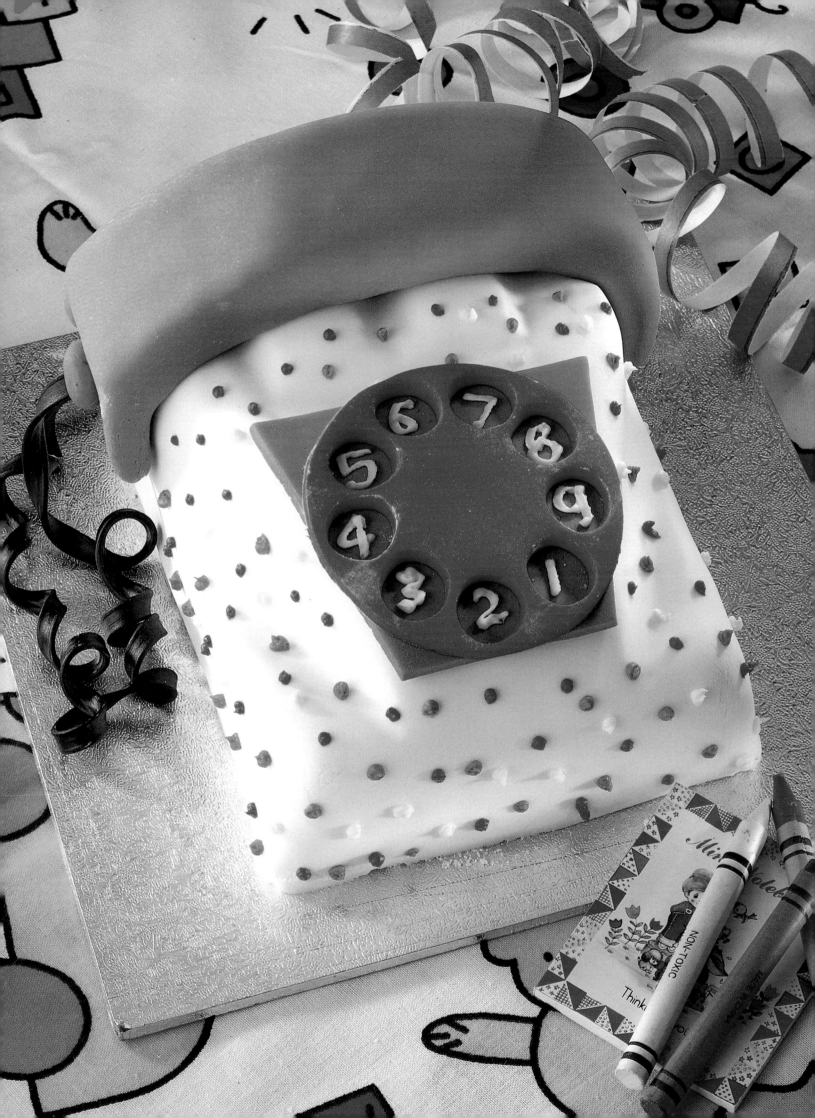

Number 7 Cake

Any combination of colors works well for this marbled cake.

INGREDIENTS
Serves 8–10
1½ x quantity Quick-Mix Sponge
Cake mix
1 quantity orange-flavor
Butter Icing
4 tbsp apricot jam, warmed and
sieved
1½ lb/2 x quantity Sugarpaste Icing
green and blue food colorings

MATERIALS AND EQUIPMENT
9 x 12 inch roasting pan
10 x 13 inch cake board
small No 7 cutter

STORING
*The finished cake can be kept in a
cool, dry place for up to three days.*

Tip

If you feel unsure about shaping
the number seven cake freehand,
you can purchase or rent shaped
cake pans from specialist cake decorating shops.

1 Preheat the oven to 350°F. Grease
the roasting pan, line the base and
sides with waxed paper and grease the
paper. Spoon the cake mixture into the
prepared pan and smooth the surface.
Bake in the center of the oven for 45–50
minutes, or until a skewer inserted into
the center of the cake comes out clean.
Leave the cake in the pan for about 5
minutes, then turn out on to a wire
rack, peel off the lining paper and leave
to cool completely.

2 ▲ Working with the cake flat side
up, lightly mark out the shape of the
number seven on the cake. Cut through
the cake, starting at the bottom end and
working up.

3 ▲ Slice through the cake
horizontally, then carefully lift off
the top layer and place on the work
surface. Place the bottom layer of cake
on the cake board and spread with the
butter icing. Reassemble the cake.

4 Brush the cake evenly with apricot
jam. Divide the sugarpaste icing
into three equal portions. Leave one
portion white, color one blue and the
last green. Cut off about 2 oz from each
of the blue and green icings, wrap each
separately in plastic wrap and set aside.
Marble the remaining blue and green
sugarpaste icing with the white
portion of icing.

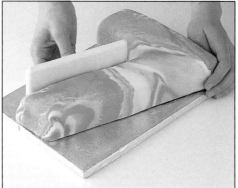

5 ▲ Roll out the marbled icing on a
work surface lightly dusted with
confectioners' sugar to a rectangle of
14 x 11 inches and use to cover the
number seven. Smooth the icing with a
cake smoother or with your hands.

6 ▲ Use the cutter to cut random
shapes out of the covered cake.
Press the cutter into the icing carefully,
but firmly. Remove the cutter and the
shape should be wedged in the cutter.
Poke out the shape with a toothpick
and discard. This stage needs to be
done immediately after the cake has
been covered, or the sugarpaste icing
will start drying out.

7 ▲ Roll out the reserved blue and
green colored sugarpaste icing and
then use the cutter to stamp out a
combination of blue and green shapes.
Use these to replace the stamped out
shapes from the cake, pressing them in
gently to fill the holes.

Valentine's Box of Chocolates

This special cake would also make a wonderful gift for Mother's Day. Choose your favorite chocolates to go inside.

INGREDIENTS
Serves 10–12
1½ x quantity chocolate-flavor
Quick-Mix Sponge Cake mix
10 oz yellow marzipan
8 tbsp apricot jam, warmed and
sieved
2 lb/2⅔ x quantity Sugarpaste Icing
red food coloring
8 oz/about 16–20 hand-made
chocolates

MATERIALS AND EQUIPMENT
heart-shaped cake pan
9 inch square piece of stiff
cardboard
9 inch square cake board
piece of string
small heart-shaped cutter
length of ribbon and a pin
paper petits fours *cases*

STORING
The finished cake can be kept in a cool, dry place for up to three days.

1 Preheat the oven to 350°F. Grease the pan, line the base with waxed paper and grease the paper. Spoon the cake mixture into the pan and smooth the surface. Bake in the center of the oven for 45–50 minutes, or until a skewer inserted into the center of the cake comes out clean. Leave the cake in the pan for about 5 minutes, then turn out on to a wire rack, peel off the lining paper and leave to cool completely.

2 ▲ Place the cake on the piece of cardboard and draw around it with a pencil. Cut the heart shape out of the cardboard and set aside. This will be used as the support for the box lid.

3 ▲ Using a large, sharp knife, cut through the cake horizontally just below where the cake starts to dome. Carefully lift the top section on to the heart-shaped cardboard and place the bottom section on the cake board.

4 Use the piece of string to measure around the outside of the bottom section of cake.

5 ▲ On a work surface lightly dusted with confectioners' sugar, roll out the marzipan into a long sausage shape to the same length as the string. Place the marzipan sausage on the cake around the outside edge. Brush the bottom and lid sections evenly with apricot jam.

6 Color the sugarpaste icing red and cut off about one-third. Cut another portion from the larger piece, about 2 oz in weight. Wrap these two portions separately in plastic wrap and set aside. On a work surface lightly dusted with confectioners' sugar, roll out the icing to a 14 inch square and use it to cover the bottom section of cake.

7 ▲ Stand the lid on a raised surface, such as a glass or bowl. Roll out the reserved one-third of sugarpaste icing to a 12 inch square and cover the lid section of the cake. Roll out the remaining piece of icing and stamp out small hearts with the cutter. Stick them around the edge of the lid with a little water. Tie the ribbon in a bow and secure on top of the lid with the pin. Carefully lift the top section on to the heart-shaped cardboard and place the bottom section on the cake board.

8 Place the chocolates in the *petits fours* cases and arrange in the bottom section of the cake. Position the lid, placing it slightly off center, to reveal the chocolates inside. Remove the ribbon and pin before serving.

ℒion Cake

For an animal lover or a celebration cake for a Leo, this cake is quick and surprisingly easy to make.

INGREDIENTS
Serves 10–15
1½ x quantity Quick-Mix Sponge
Cake mix
1 quantity orange-flavor Butter
Icing
orange and red food colorings
1½ lb yellow marzipan
2 oz/⅙ quantity Sugarpaste
Icing
red or orange liquorice strings
long and round marshmallows

MATERIALS AND EQUIPMENT
10 x 12 inch roasting pan
12 inch square cake board
cheese grater
small heart-shaped cutter

STORING
The finished cake can be kept in a cool, dry place for up to four days.

1 Preheat the oven to 350°F. Grease the roasting pan, line the base and sides with waxed paper and grease the paper. Spoon the cake mixture into the prepared pan and smooth the surface. Bake in the center of the oven for 45–50 minutes, or until a skewer inserted into the center of the cake comes out clean. Leave the cake in the pan for about 5 minutes, then turn out on to a wire rack, peel off the lining paper and leave to cool completely.

2 ▲ Place the cake, base side up, on the work surface. Use a small, sharp knife to cut around the edge of the cake in an uneven scallop design. You may need to do this several times in order to cut through to the bottom. Discard the excess cake from the edges. Turn the cake over and trim the top so that it sits squarely.

3 ▲ Place the cake on the cake board. Mix the orange-flavor butter icing in a bowl together with the orange food coloring. Spoon the butter icing on top of the cake and spread evenly over the surface and down the sides, using a small spatula.

4 On a work surface lightly dusted with confectioners' sugar, roll out about 4 oz of marzipan to a 6 inch square. Place the marzipan square in the center of the cake, gently pressing down to secure.

5 ▲ Grate the remaining marzipan on to a sheet of waxed paper. Use a spatula to lift the grated marzipan carefully on to the cake, evenly covering the sides and top up to the edges of the face panel.

6 ▲ Color the sugarpaste icing red, then roll out on a work surface dusted with confectioners' sugar. Use the heart-shaped cutter to stamp out the lion's nose and position on the cake, securing it with a little water. Take a little of the excess sugarpaste icing and use your fingers to roll out two thin strands for the mouth. Position on the cake, securing with water.

7 Cut the liquorice strings into graduated lengths, and place on the cake for the whiskers. For the eyes, flatten two round marshmallows and place on the cake, securing with water.

8 ▲ To make the eyebrows, cut the long marshmallows into 2 in lengths, and snip along one side. Place them on the cake, securing with water.

*J*ack-in-the-Box Cake

*An impressive, colorful cake which will
delight a small party of young children. This cake does
require a little extra time and patience, so be sure to start the cake
well in advance and not on the morning of the party!*

INGREDIENTS
Serves 6–8
1 quantity chocolate-flavor Quick-
Mix Sponge Cake Mix
6 tbsp apricot jam, warmed and
sieved
2¼ lb/3 x quantity Sugarpaste Icing
purple, yellow, orange and green
food colorings
1 large round doughnut
1 small round doughnut
2 marshmallow candies, for the eyes
2 colored candies, for the buttons

MATERIALS AND EQUIPMENT
*deep 4 inch square cake pan
7 inch cake board
3½ inch square piece of stiff
cardboard
3 toothpicks
garlic press
ice-cream cone
balloon
small star cutter
butterfly cutter
wooden skewer*

STORING
*The finished cake can be kept for up
to four days.*

1 Preheat the oven to 350°F. Grease the cake pan, line the base and sides with waxed paper and grease the paper. Spoon the cake mixture into the prepared pan and smooth the surface. Bake in the center of the oven for 35–40 minutes, or until a skewer inserted into the center of the cake comes out clean. Leave the cake in the pan for about 5 minutes, then turn out on to a wire rack, peel off the lining paper and leave to cool completely.

2 ▲ Place the cake on the work surface and cut a 1 inch slice off the top for the lid. Use a small, sharp knife to hollow out the center of the box section of cake, leaving a ½ inch border. Spread a little apricot jam in the center of the cake board and some on the piece of cardboard. Place the bottom section of cake on the cake board and position the lid on the cardboard. Brush the box and lid with apricot jam.

3 ▲ Pull off a walnut-sized piece of sugarpaste icing, wrap in plastic wrap and set aside. Then take about half of the remaining sugarpaste icing and marble in the purple food coloring. Cut off one-quarter of the marbled icing and roll out on a surface lightly dusted with confectioners' sugar to a 6 inch square. Use to cover the lid section, wrapping the icing around the cardboard. Set aside, cardboard side down. Reserve the trimmings.

4 Roll out the remaining marbled icing and use to cover the box section of cake, lightly pressing the icing into the hollow. Reserve the trimmings.

5 Color about half of the remaining sugarpaste icing yellow and pull off two pieces, each the size of a cherry. Wrap these in plastic wrap and set aside. Cut a thin slice off the side of the large doughnut for the body to give it a flat base. Lay it down on the work surface and place the small doughnut above it for the head. Brush the head and body with jam. Roll out the large portion of yellow sugarpaste icing until about ¼ inch thick and use to cover the head and body of the clown. Wrap the icing around the back and then pinch it together to seal.

6 ▲ Pierce a toothpick into the base of the body, leaving about half of it exposed. Place the body in position on the box section of the cake, pressing the exposed toothpick into the cake for extra stability.

7 ▲ Cut off about half of the remaining sugarpaste icing and color it orange. Push about one-quarter of this through a garlic press on to a sheet of waxed paper for the hair. Stick it on to the clown's head with a little water. Use the remaining orange icing to make one hand, the nose, mouth and a few spots for the bow tie. Allow the hand to dry out on a baking sheet, but cover the other features with plastic wrap and set aside.

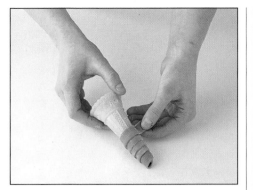

8 ▲ Color the remaining sugarpaste icing green. To make the hat, cut off about ½ oz of the green icing and roll out into a thin strip. Brush the pointed end of the ice-cream cone with a little apricot jam, then roll the strip of green sugarpaste icing around it, starting at the pointed end and working downwards. Use scissors to cut off the excess cone. Stick the hat in position on the clown's head with a little water. Reserve any trimmings.

9 Use the reserved piece of yellow sugarpaste icing to make two small ovals for the arms. Thread each one on to a toothpick and carefully press the hand on to one of them. Press the toothpicks into the body of the clown. Tie a slightly blown up balloon on to the arm without the hand.

10 Roll out the remaining piece of white sugarpaste icing and stamp out two small stars with the star cutter. Use a little water to stick them in place for the eyes. Stick the marshmallow candies on top.

11 Position the orange nose and mouth, sticking them in place with a little water. Roll out the remaining green icing to about 5mm/¼ inch thick and stamp out a butterfly and six small stars with the cutters. Stick the reserved red spots on to the butterfly bow tie, using a little water, then place the bow tie on the clown in the same way. Place the green stars around the edges of the cake board. Carefully stick the two colored candies in place for the clown's buttons, using a little more water.

12 To position the lid, carefully sit it, cardboard side out, on the back edge of the box section. Use the wooden skewer and the reserved icing trimmings to support the lid and hold it in place. This stage is best completed when the cake is in position on the table and unlikely to be moved again.

Peepo Rabbits

An easy cake to make for a chocoholic who loves rabbits.
All the fun is in the decorating.

INGREDIENTS
Serves 6–8
For the Toadstools
2 large egg whites
2 tbsp superfine sugar

For the Cake
1 quantity Jelly Roll cake mix
1 quantity chocolate-flavor Butter Icing
2½ cups shredded coconut
3 tbsp cocoa powder, plus a little extra for dusting
8 oz/⅔ quantity Sugarpaste Icing pink, yellow, green and brown food colorings

MATERIALS AND EQUIPMENT
piping bag fitted with a small round nozzle
9 x 13 inch jelly roll pan
9 inch square cake board
small rabbit cutter
small butterfly cutter
1 toothpick
small leaf cutter

STORING
The finished cake can be refrigerated for up to two days.

1 Preheat the oven to 275°F. To make the meringue toadstools, place a sheet of parchment paper on a baking sheet. Place the egg whites in a clean, dry mixing bowl and whisk until they hold soft peaks. Whisk in half of the sugar, then add the rest. Whisk until the mixture holds stiff peaks. Fill the piping bag with the meringue mixture and pipe several small rounds and several 1 inch stalks. Bake for about 1 hour, or until dry. Leave to cool completely.

2 ▲ To assemble the toadstools, gently press a stalk into a small meringue round. Set aside. Increase the oven temperature to 350°F.

3 Grease the pan, line the base and sides with waxed paper and grease the paper. Spoon the cake mixture into the pan and smooth the surface. Bake in the center of the oven for about 12 minutes, or until firm to the touch. Leave the cake in the pan, covered, to cool completely.

4 Lay a sheet of waxed paper on the work surface and sprinkle with confectioners' sugar. Tip the cake on to the waxed paper and remove the lining paper. Spread with about one-third of the butter icing and roll up. Cut off one-third of the roll and stand the larger section on the cake board, sticking it in place with a little butter icing.

5 ▲ Position the smaller log next to the larger one, then cover both in the remaining butter icing. Peak and swirl the icing quite unevenly to make it look like bark.

6 Place the coconut in a bowl and sift in the cocoa powder. Stir well until evenly blended. Spoon the coconut all around the cake.

7 ▲ Take half of the sugarpaste icing and divide into two portions. Color one portion pink. Roll out each piece on a work surface lightly dusted with confectioners' sugar until about ¼ inch thick. Stamp out two rabbits in each color. Use the pink and white trimmings to make tiny balls for the eyes, securing them in place with a little water. Place the rabbits on a baking sheet and leave until dry.

8 Cut off about one-quarter of the remaining sugarpaste icing and color it yellow. Roll out until about ¼ inch thick and stamp out a butterfly. Use the toothpick to indent the center of the butterfly gently and fold it a little. Press half of the toothpick through the base of the butterfly. Place the butterfly on the baking sheet with the rabbits, resting one wing on the edge of the baking sheet so that it dries in that position.

9 Cut off one-third of the remaining sugarpaste icing and color it green. Roll it out thinly, then cut it into strips using scissors and snip the strips into pointed sections to make the grass. Position the pieces of grass randomly in the coconut around the cake.

10 Color the remaining icing brown and roll out thinly. Cut out several leaf shapes, and then use a small, sharp knife to make the leaf indentations. Gently twist and bend the leaves a little, then place them in the coconut. Reserve the trimmings.

11 To assemble the rabbits, use a little of the reserved brown icing to stick them securely in place around the cake. Press the butterfly's toothpick into the back of the cake. Finally, position the meringue toadstools and dust them with a little cocoa powder.

A Basket of Flowers

This attractive arrangement of flowers looks very impressive, yet none of the stages are very difficult to do.

INGREDIENTS
Serves 10–12
1½ x quantity orange-flavor Quick-Mix Sponge Cake mix
2 x quantity orange-flavor Butter Icing
orange, yellow, pink, red, black and green food colorings
2 lb/2⅔ x quantity Sugarpaste Icing

MATERIALS AND EQUIPMENT
deep 8 inch round cake pan
8 inch oval cake board
3 waxed paper piping bags
small round nozzle
small straight serrated nozzle
selection of small flower and leaf cutters
12 inch piece of strong wire, bent to a curve with the two ends about 8 inch apart
plasticine

STORING
The finished cake can be kept in a cool, dry place for up to three days.

1 Preheat the oven to 350°F. Grease the cake pan, line the base with waxed paper and grease the paper. Spoon the cake mixture into the prepared pan and smooth the surface. Bake in the center of the oven for 45–50 minutes or until a skewer inserted into the center of the cake comes out clean. Turn out on to a wire rack, carefully peel off the lining paper and leave the cake to cool completely.

2 Place the butter icing in a bowl and beat in a few drops of orange food coloring. Cut the cake in half down the middle and spread the bottom of one half with a little of the butter icing. Sandwich with the other half of the cake, base to base.

3 Cut a thin slice from the bottom of the sandwiched cake. Place a little butter icing on the cake board and position the cake on top, with the large flat surface facing upwards.

4 ▲ Spread more of the butter icing over the cut surface of the cake, covering right up to the edges.

5 Place about 4 tbsp of the butter icing in a small bowl and color it with a little more orange food coloring to make it a slightly deeper color. Fit a paper piping bag with the small round nozzle and fill with the deeper orange butter icing. Pipe a decorative border around the top edge of the basket.

6 Fit the clean round nozzle into a fresh paper piping bag and fill with the lighter orange butter icing. Pipe vertical lines about 1 inch apart all around the sides of the cake. Fit a fresh paper piping bag with the serrated nozzle and fill with more orange butter icing. Starting at the top of the cake pipe short lines alternately crossing over, then stopping at the vertical lines to give a basket-weave effect.

7 Divide the sugarpaste icing into two. Cut one of the portions in half and color one half pale orange and the other half darker orange. Wrap these separately in plastic wrap and set aside. Divide the other portion of sugarpaste icing into five equal amounts. Color these yellow, pink, red, black and green.

8 ▲ Roll out the yellow, pink and red portions on a work surface lightly dusted with confectioners' sugar and use the flower cutters to stamp out the flower shapes. Place some of the flowers in an egg carton so they dry curved and place others on a baking sheet so they dry flat. Leave the flowers for at least 2 hours to dry out.

9 Use a little of the orange, yellow and black sugarpaste icings to roll into tiny balls to make the centers of the flowers, sticking them in place with a little water.

10 Roll out the green icing and use a leaf-shaped cutter to stamp out leaves, indenting them with a small, sharp knife and curling them slightly to give them more interest. Place them on the baking sheet to dry out.

11 When dry, arrange the flowers and leaves attractively on top of the basket and the cake board.

12 ▲ To make the handle for the basket, roll the two shades of orange sugarpaste icing into balls about the size of small marbles. Thread these alternately on to the curved piece of wire, leaving about 1 inch of wire exposed at each end. Stand the handle in two pieces of plasticine stuck to the work surface or a baking sheet, supported by a dish towel pushed under the handle to keep it from falling over. Leave to dry for at least 2 hours. To finish, gently press the handle into the cake, pushing it in until secure.

$\mathcal{H}$ot Dog Cake

Make a meal of a cake! This hot dog tastes nothing like the real thing - it is much more delicious and looks very attractive when cut into slices.

INGREDIENTS
Serves 6–8
1 quantity Jelly Roll mix
confectioners' sugar, to dredge
½ quantity coffee-flavor Butter Icing
⅓ quantity Truffle Cake Mix
6 tbsp apricot jam, warmed and sieved
1 lb/1⅓ x quantity Sugarpaste Icing
brown and red food colorings
1–2 tbsp toasted sesame seeds
¼ quantity Glacé Icing

MATERIALS AND EQUIPMENT
9 x 13 inch jelly roll pan
2 small waxed paper piping bags

STORING
The decorated cake should be made and served on the day.

1 Preheat the oven to 350°F. Grease the pan, line the base and sides with waxed paper and grease the paper. Spoon the cake mixture into the pan and smooth the surface. Bake in the center of the oven for about 12 minutes or until springy to the touch. Cover and leave to cool.

2 Turn the cake out on to waxed paper dusted with confectioners' sugar and remove the lining paper. Spread over the butter icing, then roll the cake up using the waxed paper.

3 ▲ Shape the truffle cake mix into a sausage about 9 inches long.

4 Place the jelly roll on the work surface and slice along the middle lengthwise, almost through to the bottom. Ease the two halves apart to resemble a partially opened bun.

5 Color the sugarpaste icing brown, then cut off about 2 oz and set aside, wrapped in plastic wrap. Roll out the rest on a work surface lightly dusted with confectioners' sugar until about ¼ inch thick and use to cover the bun. Ease the icing into the center and down the sides of the cake.

6 ▲ Dilute a few drops of brown food coloring in a little water and paint the top of the bun very lightly to give a toasted effect. Dab on a little color, then rub it around gently with a finger until blended in. Carefully place the truffle cake sausage in position.

7 ▲ Divide the glacé icing between two small bowls. Color one half brown and the other red. Fill the piping bags with the icings and snip off the ends with scissors. Pipe red icing along the sausage for the ketchup, then overlay with brown icing for the mustard. Sprinkle the sesame seeds over the bun.

8 Roll out the reserved brown sugarpaste icing and cut thin strips to resemble onion rings. Place on the cake so that the joins lie under the sausage. Carefully place the cake on a napkin and serving plate, with a knife and fork.

 alloween Coffin

A simple, spooky cake for the centerpiece of a Halloween party.

INGREDIENTS
Serves 4–6
1 quantity Quick-Mix Sponge Cake mix
5 tbsp apricot jam, warmed and sieved
12 oz/1 quantity Sugarpaste Icing
black food coloring
3 oz yellow marzipan
¼ quantity Butter Icing
golden superfine sugar, for dusting

MATERIALS AND EQUIPMENT
2 lb loaf pan
9 inch square piece of thick cardboard
small fluted oval cutter
small plastic skeleton and other Halloween toys
piping bag fitted with a small star nozzle

STORING
The finished cake can be made up to two days in advance and kept in a cool, dry place.

1 Preheat the oven to 350°F. Grease the pan, line the base and sides with waxed paper and grease the paper. Spoon the mixture into the pan and smooth the surface. Bake in the center of the oven for 35–40 minutes, or until a skewer inserted into the cake comes out clean. Leave the cake in the pan for 5 minutes, then turn out on to a wire rack, peel off the lining paper and leave to cool.

2 To shape the cake, use a large, sharp knife to slice off the risen surface to make it completely flat. Turn the cake upside-down and score the shape of the coffin in the cake. Cut off the two top corners at an angle, then cut diagonally down from the corners to the base of the coffin.

3 ▲ To make the lid of the coffin, slice about ½ inch off the top of the cake. To make a base to reinforce the coffin and lid, place both pieces of cake on the cardboard and draw around them with a pencil. Remove the cakes and cut out the shapes on the cardboard. Brush the cakes with apricot jam.

4 Use a small, sharp knife to hollow out the base of the coffin, leaving about a ½ inch border. Place the coffin and lid on the cards. Brush the cakes with apricot jam.

5 Color the sugarpaste icing black, then cut off about one-third and set aside, wrapped in plastic wrap. Roll out the larger portion of sugarpaste icing on a work surface lightly dusted with confectioners' sugar and use to cover the base of the coffin, easing it into the hollow and down the sides. Trim the edges. Roll out the remaining black icing and cover the lid. Trim the edges.

6 ▲ To make the coffin handles, pull off six small pieces of the marzipan and shape into sausages with rounded ends. To make the plaque on the lid, roll out the kneaded trimmings of marzipan thinly and stamp out a fluted oval with the cutter. Stick the handles and plaque in position with a little butter icing.

7 Lay the skeleton in the coffin. Color the remaining butter icing black and use to pipe a small star border around the coffin and down the sides. Sprinkle with sifted superfine sugar and decorate with the Halloween toys.

Mermaid Cake

Pretty, elegant and chocolatey! Every little girl's dream.

INGREDIENTS
Serves 6–8
1 quantity chocolate-flavor Quick-
Mix Sponge Cake mix
1 lb plain chocolate
3 cups unsalted, unflavored popcorn
1 lb/1⅓ x quantity Sugarpaste Icing
lilac and pink food colorings
3 tbsp apricot jam, warmed and
sieved
1 egg white, lightly beaten
raw sugar, for the sand

MATERIALS AND EQUIPMENT
2 lb loaf pan
12 x 6 inch cake board
doll, similar in dimensions to a
"Barbie" or "Sindy" doll
small crescent-shaped cutter
small fluted round cutter
6 inch piece of thin lilac ribbon

STORING
*The finished cake can be made up to
three days in advance and kept in a
cool, dry place.*

 Tip

For an even more chocolatey version of this cake, cut the sponge into three horizontally and use 1 quantity chocolate-flavor Butter Icing to spread between the layers. Reassemble the cake and then cover with chocolate popcorn.

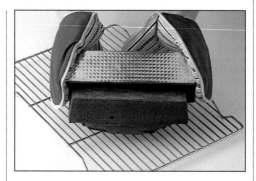

1 ▲ Preheat the oven to 350°F. Grease the pan, line the base and sides with waxed paper and grease the paper. Spoon the cake mixture into the prepared pan and smooth the surface. Bake in the center of the oven for 35–40 minutes, or until a skewer inserted into the center of the cake comes out clean. Leave the cake in the pan for about 5 minutes, then turn out on to a wire rack, peel off the lining paper and leave to cool.

2 ▲ Turn the cake dome side up and place on the cake board. Melt the chocolate in a bowl placed over hot water. Add the popcorn and stir until evenly coated. Spoon the popcorn around the sides of the cake and on the cake board. Spread any remaining melted chocolate over the top of the cake until evenly covered. Set aside at room temperature.

3 Cut off about one-quarter of the sugarpaste icing. Color the larger piece lilac and the smaller piece pink. Cut off about one-third of the lilac icing, wrap this and the pink icing separately in plastic wrap and set aside.

4 ▲ On a work surface lightly dusted with confectioners' sugar, roll out the larger portion of lilac sugarpaste icing to an oblong shape wide enough to wrap around the doll's legs and about 2 inches longer. Brush the doll from the waist down with the apricot jam, then wrap her in the sugarpaste icing, lightly pinching and squeezing it around her legs to make it stick. Working downwards towards her feet, pinch the end of the tail to form a fin shape, curling the ends slightly.

5 ▲ Position the mermaid on the cake, moving her slightly until she feels secure and then pressing down firmly. Roll out the reserved lilac and pink sugarpaste icing and use the crescent-shaped cutter to stamp out the scales. Cover the scales and the reserved trimmings with plastic wrap to prevent them drying out. Starting at the fin end of the tail, brush the scales with a tiny amount of egg white and stick on to the tail, overlapping all the time, until the tail is completely covered.

6 Re-roll the reserved icing trimmings and use the small fluted cutter to stamp out a shell-shaped bra top for the mermaid. Make indentations on the top with the back of a knife, then stick in place with a little extra apricot jam. Use the ribbon to tie up the mermaid's hair.

7 Position the cake on the serving table or large board, then scatter the raw sugar around the base of the cake for the sand and add a few real shells, if you like. Remove the doll before serving the cake.

Helicopter Cake

Perfect for a party of boys or girls who are partial to helicopters.
The cake involves a little creative use of non-edible items which
must be removed before eating.

INGREDIENTS
Serves 6–8
1 quantity Quick-Mix Sponge Cake
mix
2 fan wafers
6–8 tbsp apricot jam, warmed and
sieved
12 oz/1 quantity Sugarpaste Icing
red, blue and black food colorings
small round candy
¼ quantity Butter Icing
2 candies, for the headlights
2 x 6 inch pieces of flat
liquorice
4 x 1 inch pieces of liquorice sticks
1 cup shredded coconut, toasted

MATERIALS AND EQUIPMENT
2 lb loaf pan
small round cutter
2 wooden skewers
wood glue
small wooden block, to raise
helicopter
7 inch square cake board
5 inch piece of white ribbon
piping bag fitted with a small plain
nozzle

STORING
The finished cake can be kept in a
cool, dry place for up to two days.

1 Preheat the oven to 350°F. Grease the pan, line with waxed paper and grease the paper. Spoon the cake mixture into the prepared pan and smooth the surface. Bake in the center of the oven for 35–40 minutes, or until a skewer inserted into the center of the cake comes out clean. Turn out on to a wire rack, peel off the lining paper and leave to cool.

2 ▲ To shape the cake, stand it flat side down and use a large, sharp knife to cut it into the shape of a teardrop. Trim the sides from top to bottom so that the top is wider than the bottom. Turn the cake on its side, and cut a wedge shape out of the back part.

3 ▲ Invert the cake so that the flat side is uppermost. Use the round cutter to stamp out a hole for the cockpit, indenting about 1 inch. Remove the round piece and reserve.

4 Cut a thin slice from each of the wafers, reserve one for the tail fin and discard the other slice. Cut each wafer in half lengthwise. Measure the long side of one of the wafers and then cut the wooden skewers double that length. Glue the skewers together in the center to form a cross and set aside.

5 Remove a small piece of sugarpaste icing. Take another piece of icing about the size of an egg and color it deep blue. Wrap these pieces in plastic wrap and set aside.

6 Color the remaining sugarpaste icing pale blue. Remove an egg-sized piece, wrap in plastic wrap and set aside. Brush the cake with jam. Roll out the pale blue sugarpaste on a work surface dusted with confectioners' sugar and use to cover the helicopter. Position the covered cake on the small block of wood on the cake board.

7 To make the propeller support, brush the reserved piece of round cake cut out for the pilot's cockpit with apricot jam. Roll out the reserved pale blue sugarpaste icing and cover the round cake. Reserve the trimmings. Position the propeller support on the helicopter, half way between the cockpit and the tail, sticking it in place with a dab of jam. Place the crossed skewers on top of the propeller support and secure them in place with a little of the pale blue icing. Place the wafers over the skewers, securing them underneath with more icing. Place the small round candy on top.

8 ▲ To make the pilot, shape the dark blue sugarpaste icing into a small head and body to fit into the cockpit. Color a little of the reserved white icing red for the nose and mouth and use white icing for the buttons. Stick the details in place with a little water. Shape some of the reserved pale blue icing into the pilot's hat and place on his head, securing with a little water if necessary. Sit the pilot in his seat and tie the ribbon scarf around his neck.

9 Color the butter icing black and fill the piping bag. First pipe in the pilot's eyes, then pipe the zigzag and straight borders around the helicopter. Stick the headlight candies in position with a little of the remaining butter icing and stick the tail fin on in the same way. To make the landing feet, smooth out the flat pieces of liquorice and fold in half lengthwise. Position on the cake board, wedged in with the liquorice sticks. Scatter the shredded coconut around the cake board.

Banjo Cake

The perfect cake for the musician in the family. It can be set on a tray or you could cut out cardboard for a template to support it.

INGREDIENTS
Serves 15–20
2 x quantity Quick-Mix Sponge
Cake mix
6 tbsp seedless raspberry jam,
warmed
2 lb/2²/₃ x quantity Sugarpaste Icing
lime green food coloring
2 colored liquorice sticks
4 round lollipops
4 tbsp colored jimmies
piece of flat green liquorice
2 long red liquorice strings
4 long green liquorice strings
sugarpaste stars, or other decoration

MATERIALS AND EQUIPMENT
8 inch round cake pan
7 inch square cake pan
21 inch stiff cardboard
2 inch round cutter
ribbon and 2 pins, for the strap

STORING
The finished cake can be made up to two days in advance and kept in a cool, dry place.

1 Preheat the oven to 350°F. Grease the pans, line the bases with waxed paper and grease the paper. Divide the cake mixture between the two pans and smooth the surfaces. Bake for 35–40 minutes, or until firm to the touch. Turn out on to a wire rack, peel off the lining paper and then leave to cool completely.

2 ▲ Cut off the dome from the round cake and place bottom side up on the work surface. Cut the dome off the square cake, then cut in half down the middle. Place the cakes together to form the banjo shape, then draw around them on to stiff cardboard. Cut out the shape to make the reinforcing template.

3 ▲ Use the cutter to stamp out a shallow hollow from the center of the round cake. Place both cakes on the cardboard base and brush with the raspberry jam. Color the sugarpaste icing with the lime green food coloring and roll out on a work surface lightly dusted with confectioners' sugar to about a 25 x 10 inch rectangle. Use to cover the banjo in one piece, easing the icing into the hollow and down the sides. Make finger indentations along the length of the neck of the banjo.

4 Cut off four ½ inch pieces from one of the liquorice sticks and press into the cake at the top end of the neck to resemble stays for the strings. Place the remains of the liquorice stick with the other one at the base of the banjo, next to the hollow. Dip the lollipops in water, then in the colored jimmies to coat. Press the lollipops into the sides of the neck end so that they line up with the pieces of liquorice stick forming the stays.

5 Place the two flat pieces of liquorice side by side at the base, securing with a little water. Cut the red liquorice strings into about 2 inch lengths and position them along the length of the banjo neck, in the indentations. Use a little water to stick them securely in place, if necessary.

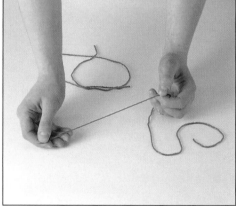

6 ▲ Dip the green liquorice strings in hot water, then stretch and smooth each one until perfectly straight. Wrap one end of the banjo strings around the liquorice sticks at the top of the neck end and bring the other ends down so they meet together on the flat liquorice at the rounded end. Secure the ribbon strap with pins pushed through each end and into the cake. Decorate the banjo with sugarpaste stars and more colored jimmies, if wished. The pins *must* be removed from the cake before serving.

Index

A
Almonds
    almond and apricot cake, 93
    carrot and almond cake, 90
Apples, marzipan, 54
Apricots
    almond and apricot cake, 93
    lemon and apricot cake, 88

B
Baking equipment, 8, 9
Balloon whisks, 8
Banana coconut cake, 92
Bananas, marzipan, 54
Banjo cake, 156
Basket of flowers, 148
Basket-weave
    butter icing, 60
    marzipan, 56
Beads, piping, 39
Birthday bowl of strawberries, 126
Birthday present, 122
Black forest gâteau, 98
Blossoms, marzipan, 53
Bluebird bon voyage cake, 110
Borders, cut-out, 48
Bought decorations, using, 74-81
Braid, marzipan, 56
Bunch of grapes, marzipan, 54
Butter icing
    cake sides, on, 58
    cake tops, on, 59
    decorating with, 58-61
    diamonds, 59
    feathered spiral, 59
    flavorings, 26
    piping with, 60
    recipe, 26
    ridged spiral, 59

    ridged squares, 59
    swirls, 59

C
Cake boards, 9
Cake pans, 9
    deep round, lining, 19
    lining, 19
    shallow round, lining, 19
Candy flowers, 76
Candy-stripe rope, marzipan, 56
Carrot and almond cake, 90
Cat on a mat, modelling, 46
Cherries
    Black forest gâteau, 98
    cherry batter cake, 89
Chestnuts
    chocolate chestnut roulade, 102
Chili peppers, marzipan, 54
Chocolate
    Black forest gâteau, 98
    butter icing, flavoring, 26
    chocolate chestnut roulade, 102
    coating cakes with, 66
    curls, 71
    cut-outs, 70
    decorating with, 66-71
    fruit and nuts, dipped, 71
    lace curls, 67
    leaves, 70
    marbling, 68
    melting, 66
    outlines, 67
    piping with, 67
    quick-mix sponge cake, 10
    run-outs, 68
    satin chocolate icing, 29
    shavings, 71
    vegan chocolate gâteau, 100
Chocolate-iced anniversary cake, 123
Christening cake, daisy, 106
Christmas tree cake, 116
Citrus
    butter icing, flavoring, 26
    quick-mix sponge cake, 10
Cobweb icing, 62
Coconut
    banana coconut cake, 92
    ducks on a pond, 130
    peepo rabbits, 146
Coffee
    butter icing, flavoring, 26
Coloring
    flicking, 72
    linework, 72
    painting and drawing, 73
    powdered tints, 73
    stencils, using, 72
    stippling, 73

Coloring icings, 35
Cornelli, piping, 38
Crimping
    marzipan, with, 52
    sugarpaste, with, 45
Crimping tools, 20
Curls
    chocolate, 71
    multiple, 78
    ribbon, 78
Cut-outs, chocolate, 70
Cutters, 21

D
Daisy christening cake, 106
Decorating equipment, 20, 21
Diamonds
    butter icing, 59
Dots, piping, 39
Drawing, 73
Ducks on a pond, 130
Dump truck, 132

E
Easter egg nest cake, 119
Edible decorations, 74
Electric beaters, 8
Embossing
    marzipan, with, 52
    sugarpaste, with, 45
Embroidery, piping, 38
Exotic celebration gâteau, 101

F
Fan icing, 63
Feather icing, 63
Flicking, 72
Florists' wire, tape and stamens, 20
Flourless fruit cake, 86
Flower nail, 20
Flowers
    marbling, 64
    piping, 41
    sugar-frosting, 80
Frills, sugarpaste, 50
Fruit
    chocolate-dipped, 71
    sugar-frosting, 80, 81
Fruit cake, flourless, 86
Fudge frosting, recipe, 28
Fudge-frosted starry roll, 112

G
Glacé icing
    cobweb, 62
    decorating with, 62-64
    fan, 63
    feather, 63
    flowers and leaves, marbling, 64

recipe, 27
squiggle, 64
Golden wedding heart cake, 124
Gooseberry cake, 87
Greaseproof paper, 8

H
Halloween coffin, 151
Halloween pumpkin patch, 118
Helicopter cake, 154
Hot dog cake, 150

I
Iced fancies, 84
Icing
  awkward shapes, 34
  coloring, 35
  square cake, 33
Icing turntable, 20

J
Jack-in-the-box cake, 144
Jelly roll
  fudge-frosted starry roll, 112
  hot dog cake, 150
  peepo rabbits, 146
  recipe, 11
  pan, lining, 19
Jewel cake, 94

L
Leaves
  chocolate, 70
  marbling, 64
  marzipan, 53
  piping, 38
Lemon and apricot cake, 88
Light fruit cake
  quantities chart, 17
  recipe, 16
Lines, piping, 39
Linework, 72
Lion cake, 142
Loops, ribbon, 78
Lucky horseshoe, 114

M
Madeira cake
  birthday bowl of strawberries, 126
  birthday present, 122
  bluebird bon voyage cake, 110
  chocolate-iced anniversary cake, 123
  quantities chart, 13
  recipe, 12
Marbling, 44
  chocolate, 68
  flowers and leaves 68
Marzipan
  applying for sugarpaste icing, 30

basket-weave, 56
braid, 56
braiding and weaving, 56
bunch of grapes, 54
candy-stripe rope, 56
colorful blossoms, 53
crimping, 52
cut-outs, 53
decorating with, 52-57
embossing, 52
frilly blossoms and leaves, 53
modeling with, 54
recipe, 22
ripe bananas, 54
roses, 57
rosy apples, 54
royal icing, applying to round
  cake for, 31
storing, 22
twist, 56
using, 22
violets, 53
Measuring cup, 8
Measuring spoons, 8
Mermaid cake, 152
Metal spoons, 8
Modeling
  sugarpaste, with, 46

N
Nozzle brush, 20
Nozzles, 20
Number 7 cake, 138
Nuts
  chocolate-dipped, 71

O
One-stage Victoria sandwich, 84
Ovals, ribbon, 78
Oven gloves, 9

P
Paintbrushes, 20
Painting, 73
Pansy, piping, 41
Papers, 21
Patterns with edible decorations, 74
Peepo rabbits, 146
Piping
  beads, 39
  butter icing, with, 60
  chocolate, with, 67
  cornelli, 38
  dots, 39
  leaves, 38
  lines, 39
  pansy, 41
  rose, 41
  royal icing, with, 36-42

run-outs, 42
scrolls, 38
shells, 39
simple embroidery, 38
stars, 38
sugar pieces, 40
summer flowers, 41
swirls, 38
trellises, 39
twisted ropes, 38
zigzags, 39
Piping bags
  making, 36, 37
  using, 36, 37
Plaques, sugarpaste, 51
Plastic scrapers, 20
Plunger blossoms, 49
Powdered tints, 73

Q
Quick-mix sponge cake
  banjo cake, 156
  basket of flowers, 148
  chocolate, 10
  citrus, 10
  ducks on a pond, 130
  dump truck, 132
  Easter egg nest cake, 119
  Halloween coffin, 151
  Halloween pumpkin patch, 118
  helicopter cake, 154
  Jack-in-the-box cake, 144
  lion cake, 142
  mermaid cake, 152
  number 7 cake, 138
  recipe, 10
  telephone cake, 136
  train cake, 134
  Valentine's box of chocolates, 140

R
Rabbit, modeling, 46
Ribbons
   curls, 78
   decorations, 78
   designs, 78
   insertion, 78
   loops, 78
   multiple curls, 78
   ovals, 78
Rich fruit cake
   Christmas tree cake, 116
   daisy christening cake, 106
   golden wedding heart cake, 124
   lucky horseshoe, 114
   quantities chart, 15
   recipe, 14
   rose blossom wedding cake, 108
Rolling pins, 20
Ropes
   twisted, piping, 38
Rose
   marzipan, 57
   piping, 41
Rose blossom wedding cake, 108
Rough icing, 33
Royal icing
   colored, 42
   consistency, 25
   covering round cake with, 32
   decorating with, 36-42
   flat icing with, 25
   marzipanning round cake for, 31
   peaking, for, 25
   piping, for, 25
   piping with, 36-42
   recipe, 24
   run-outs, for, 25
   storing, 24
Run-outs, 42
   chocolate, 68

S
Satin chocolate icing, 29
Scales, 8
Scrolls, piping, 38
Shapes, cut-out, 48
Shells, piping, 39
Sifters, 8
Simnel cake, 97
Snowman, modeling, 46
Spatulas, 9
Spirals
   butter icing, 59
Squares
   butter icing, 59
Squiggle icing, 64
Stars, piping, 38
Stenciling, 76

Stencils, 72
Stippling, 73
Straight-edge ruler, 20
Strawberry cream gâteau, 96
Sugar pieces, piped, 40
Sugar-frosting flowers and fruit, 80, 81
Sugarpaste icing
   cat on a mat, 46
   covering with, 34
   crimping, 45
   cut-out borders, 48
   cut-out shapes, 48
   decorating with, 44-51
   embossing, 45
   frills, 50
   frosty snowman, 46
   hungry rabbit, 46
   marbling, 44
   marzipanning cake for, 30
   modeling with, 46
   plaques, 51
   plunger blossoms, 49
   recipe, 23
   smart teddy bear, 46
Swirls
   butter icing, 59
   piping, 38

T
Teddy bear, modeling, 46
Telephone cake, 136
Train cake, 134
Trellises, piping, 39
Truffle cake
   hot dog cake, 150
   recipe, 18
Twist, marzipan, 56

V
Valentine's box of chocolates, 140
Vegan chocolate gâteau, 100
Victoria sandwich, one-stage, 84
Violets, marzipan, 53

W
Wedding cake, rose blossom, 108
Wire racks, 9
Wooden spoons, 8

Z
Zigzags, piping, 39

Acknowledgements
Angela Nilsen would like to thank the Stork Cookery Service for the Rich Fruit Cake chart and Jackie Mason for her invaluable help. Sarah Maxwell would like to thank Scenics Cake Boards and Colours Direct (081–441 3082) and the Cloth Store (0293 560943), for supplying props and materials, and Braun and Kenwood for the use of their equipment.